LIVING THROUGH SOVIET TIMES

A Ukrainian family's 20th Century odyssey

Edited by

Tatiana V. Kramchaninova-Serebrovska
and
John T. Reeves

D1600194

Living Through Soviet Times
Published through IngramSparks

All rights reserved
Copyright © by Tatiana V. Kramchaninova-Serebrovska and John T. Reeves
Cover art copyright © by Tatiana V. Kramchaninova-Serebrovska

Library of Congress Catalog Number: 2021905678

ISBN: 978-1-7366516-0-5 (Paperback Edition)
ISBN: 978-1-7366516-1-2 (eBook Edition)

No part of this publication may be reproduced, stored in a retrieval system, or transmitted in any form or by any means electronic, mechanical, photocopying, recording, or otherwise, without the written permission of the author of publisher.

To the millions of Ukrainians whose stories will never be told,

and

to Allied airmen lost in World War II, including WWR Jr.,
brother of JTR.

TABLE OF CONTENTS

ILLUSTRATIONS

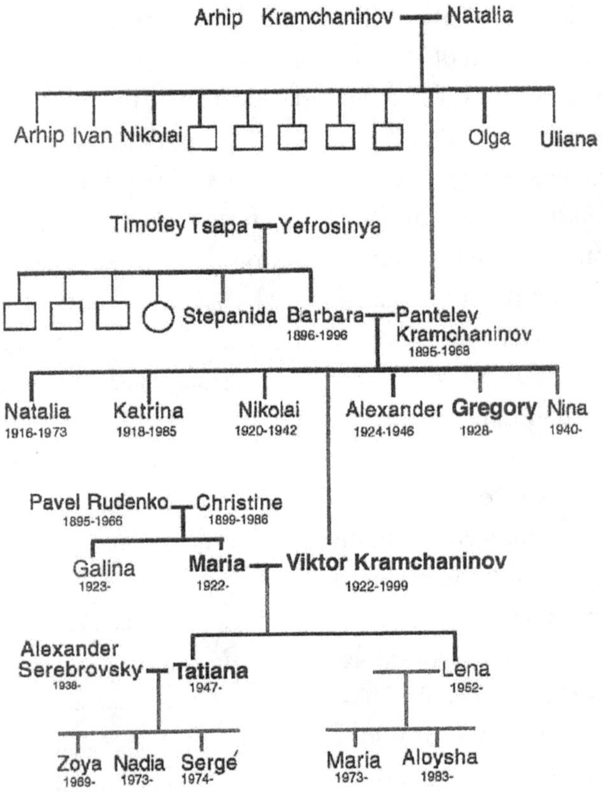

Family tree, abridged, showing generations from Viktor's grandparents to his grandchildren. Where known, dates of birth and death are shown. Where names are not known, males are shown as rectangles and females as circles.

Geographical sketch of Ukraine. In the west, the broken line running south from Belorus represents the 1938 border between Ukraine and Poland.

PREFACE

My father, Viktor Kramchaninov, would be pleased, but very surprised that his memoirs are published. In 1985, he began writing his life's history for his children, grandchildren, and future descendants. He never considered a wider audience. So just imagine how great would be his surprise if he knew that his Cyrillic script had become English print and had made the journey westward from his Kiev apartment across Europe and the Atlantic to the United States.

I wish I could tell him the full story of how it happened. Some events he knew, even though he couldn't have imagined that each event would be a step on the way to this book. He saw the disintegration in 1989 of the "iron curtain," and knew that ordinary Soviet citizens such as myself could now travel abroad. He was proud that I had been invited to Japan in August 1991 for the International Symposium on High-Altitude Medical Science, my first trip beyond Soviet borders. I had told him that of the dozens of well-known scientists from many countries, I had been very surprised that one of them, John (Jack) Reeves, a prominent cardiologist and physiologist from the U.S.A., had a vivid interest in the life of Ukraine. While some of the other participants knew nothing of my country, Jack wanted to know in detail the reasons and consequences of our separation from the Soviet Union, which our president had announced barely a week before. Then, eighteen months later, when Jack came to Ukraine, he and Father met.

At first sight, these two extraordinary men became cordial friends. Although Jack knew little Ukrainian, and Father, only some German and Spanish, words seemed unnecessary for mutual understanding. On one visit in bitterly cold weather, Jack wore Father's long winter underwear and ate his prized hot fish soup. Warm long johns and hot soup are underrated but effective ways to build friendships. In Ukraine we say, "One mountain doesn't move to join another, but friendship brings men together." Father and Jack spoke more by the heart than by the tongue. Father knew that surprising events had brought the two of them together across barriers of language, chasms of cultural difference, and eight thousand miles of separation. But he did not know that these events were steps toward publication of his memoirs.

In 1999, Jack visited Father, who was then on his deathbed, and on that visit he asked me to send him a translation of Father's memoirs. Expressing Father's thoughts in English required late nights over many months, but it was a labor of love to salve a daughter's grief. After the translation was done, Jack told me that this narrative could help Americans understand what we Ukrainians had experienced. We began to ponder publication, but soon realized the story was incomplete. Because father never completed his memoirs, and because other voices were needed, Jack had Maria, my mother, Viktor's brother, Gregory, and myself, each tell our own stories. When Jack read these, he came to believe that the various experiences of our family were vignettes of momentous Soviet events. Jack saw how Father had struggled with Communist doctrine. Father's lifelong journey from faith to doubt was a thread running through the entire narrative of his memoirs, and could be an illustration for future generations of why Soviet Communism arose, why it long persisted, and why it fell. Jack assembled accounts, arranged them for Western readers, and checked every detail to ensure that the text captured the intent, emotion, and style of our narratives. When the family gathered for holidays and festive occasions, I read sentence by sentence, re-translating the text from English back into Russian, to ensure that our collective memories were authentic.

I hope that these memoirs provide a clear, fresh, and personal window through which people in the West will better understand our history. In my four visits to the United States and Canada since Ukraine became independent, I have seen that Americans are not so aware of Ukrainian life during Soviet times. And how could they know? We were a closed society for nearly seventy years. I have seen that what is absolutely obvious to us can be incomprehensible to my Western friends. Maybe this simple narrative illustrating lives of ordinary Ukrainians can help people of two continents better understand one another. After all, understanding is the foundation for friendship. At long last, we humans are really beginning to believe that we live on the same little planet called Earth, take in the same air, are sick with the same diseases and dream the same lofty dreams. We say, "Riches are not a hundred rubles, but a hundred friends." I want this book to promote Ukrainian-American understanding and, through understanding, friendship.

Tatiana Kramchaninova-Serebrovska

ACKNOWLEDGEMENTS

Alexander Serebrovsky provided important comments and historical information. In addition, we acknowledge the helpful comments of many readers: Catherine Anderson, Marta Arnold, Eric Baker, Howard and Ann Bray, Tim Brooks, Banks Clark, Charlotte Clark, Mary Conroy, Neil Davie, Joann Davies, A.A. Fickle, Robert F. Grover, Amy Hecht, Lt. S. Lopez, Kenneth Morris, Rebecca Pyle, Carol Reeves, R.J. Ruffle, Ania Savage, Zoya Serebrovska, Scott Torgenson, and C.T. Young. Personnel at the Denver Public Library were extremely helpful in obtaining resource material. We particularly are grateful to Ailsa Sinclair Davie and Jasmine Trinks who repeatedly read and copyedited the manuscript prior to its final submission. After Jack's death in 2004, Jack's three daughters, Charlotte Clark, Catherine Anderson, and Beth Reeves worked hard to finalize the publication; and two of Jack's grandchildren, Sterling Anderson and Banks Clark, drafted front and back cover ideas. Photographs and personal letters are from the Kramchaninov family album. Selections of Viktor Kramchaninov's favorite poems, which introduce the chapters, the maps and the chronology of national and international events, were prepared by the editors.

INTRODUCTION

The birth, life, and death of the Soviet Union, taken together, may be the principal events of world history in the twentieth century. How did it happen that millions would have their hopes raised, sustained, and then dashed? Following the 1917 "October Revolution," popular support for Soviet Communism grew into an enormous experiment. By the final decade of the century, the experiment had failed and the Soviet Union had been dissolved. The intervening, tumultuous seven decades saw Stalin's assumption of power and his collectivization of agriculture, followed by famines, purges, World War II, the Soviet incursion into Afghanistan, the nuclear accident at Chernobyl, Ukrainian independence, and economic depression. For decades the Soviet people obeyed the laws, farmed the land, fought the battles, and suffered abuse, poverty and hunger – believing that with persistence, they would ultimately become the happiest people on earth. These memoirs by Viktor Kramchaninov and his family tell of their beliefs, hopes and feelings and also of their struggles, both for survival and with Communist Party dogma. The Kramchaninov family paint a picture of life before, during, and after Soviet times.

Life was hard. It was hard for Viktor Kramchaninov's father in the early 1900s, and for his grandfather in the late 1800s. Like their forebears, Viktor's parent, Panteley and Varvara, had to farm and mine coal just to survive (Chapter 1). Their home, the Donbass region in eastern Ukraine, got its name from the Donets River basin, "Donets Bassein," which was and is home to huge coal deposits and extensive iron and steel manufacturing plants. The hard life of Viktor's parents was made worse by the turmoil that followed Russia's 1914 entry into World War I. The enormous losses in that war, the abdication in 1917 of Czar Nicholas II, the 1917 Bolshevik Revolution, and the bloody Civil War involving mainly the Reds

(Bolsheviks) and Whites (anti-Communists) all followed in quick succession. With war, famine, and disease compounding generation after generation of endless drudgery, Viktor's parents welcomed a bright new era of hope promised by Lenin's communism. Everyone would work together and all would have bread. By 1922, with war and famine ending, Viktor's parents embraced his birth and the official birth of their country, the Soviet Union. Fortuitously, Maria, Viktor's future wife, was born the same year.

Until 1929, Viktor's family lived and worked in a relatively stable setting. But then, Viktor's father was among the "twenty thousand," who formed the first wave of those ordered by Stalin to collective farms. Viktor's father became manager for one of the first of the collective farms (Chapter 2), and Maria's father worked in others (Chapter 5). During the famine of 1931-1933, both men ran afoul of restrictive government policies, and were sent to prison for more than a year, leaving their families to cope with threatening starvation as best they could (Chapters 3,5)

However, Victor and Maria were soon separated by circumstances beyond their control; the war began and Victor proudly joined the Soviet Air Fleet (Chapter 6). Victor experienced an insider view of the harrowing secret flight to the United States by Soviet Foreign Minister Molotov to meet with President Franklin D. Roosevelt (Chapter 7). Soon after, Victor began running bombing missions and writes of his successes and breathtaking close calls with death fighting the German army (Chapter 8) surviving two crash landing behind enemy lines, rescue and rehabilitation by "Partisans," local sympathizers, return to Soviet territory where he resumed bombing air raids, and the victorious end to the war (Chapter 9).

Concurrently, during the war, Maria fled their town of L'viv as it fell to the Germans, avoiding deportation to German labor camps by feigning illness, battled rheumatic fever after working through the winter at a collective farm, and endeavored to continue her medical studies (Chapter 10). Victor's younger brother, Gregory, provides another perspective on the war describing how the Kramchaninov family survived four years of German occupation in Zhitomyr (Chapter 11).

Life after the war is described by Maria in the joyous context of her marriage to Victor and birth of their first child, Tatiana (Chapter 12), and by Viktor in the context of a deep depression that only Maria's love and care could cure (Chapter 13).

Following Stalin's death in 1953, and under a succession of Party secretaries, Soviet society, and Viktor and Maria's family, saw a slowly increasing economic security, a greater educational opportunity, and an erratically increasing freedom of expression (Chapter 14). Welcome as these were, they were accompanied by a growing awareness, within the family and in the nation, of Stalin's abuses and of subsequent failings of the central Soviet government. Viktor, however, was a staunch patriot, and was brought up in school idolizing Stalin During the war he went into battle absolutely sincerely with the words "For the Motherland, for Stalin.» In the 1950s and 1960s, Viktor, who was a staunch patriot, refused to believe that Stalin had cruelly executed Soviet citizens as claimed by Khrushchev. Eventually, several activities began to crack Viktor's strong belief in the political structure of the Soviet Union. First, after reading a huge amount of literature, including Solzhenitsyn and Vasily Grossman, my father realized how terribly the Communist Party had deceived his generation. Second, in the 1970's, a confrontation from within his family revealed that relatives of his own son-in-law had been murdered in Stalin's Purges of 1937 (Chapter 14). This exposure by Khrushchev of the personality cult of Stalin was personally devastating for Viktor. He wrote little about this time in the memoirs, and for several years was very worried, saying: "So what happens, we went to death with his name in vain?"

In 1981, Viktor's brother Gregory, a Soviet advisor in Afghanistan, brought back disturbing experiences, suggesting that the Soviet leaders had blundered into a costly, unwinnable war (Chapter 15). However, beliefs from early childhood, as well as those instilled by years of pro-Soviet propaganda, are not often reversed by hearing the experiences of others.

For Viktor, the crisis of belief came in 1986 when he saw with his own eyes the government's response to the massive nuclear accident at Chernobyl (Chapter 16). He observed that Soviet officials deliberately delayed a public announcement of the catastrophe for a week—until their own children had been safely evacuated. By refusing to publicize the explosion and fire at the Chernobyl reactor, the government caused the exposure of hundreds of thousands of ordinary citizens and their children to dangerous and unprecedented amounts of radioactive fallout. Viktor's own family had been exposed to extraordinarily high levels of radiation. The Chernobyl nuclear accident caused Viktor to realize for the first time that the Soviet government had contempt for its own people. As he said, he had been "treated like a condom which the government had used and then thrown away." Now he finally understood and accepted that the abuses of Stalin had really occurred and that, though lessened, governmental abuses continued in subsequent years (Chapter 16).

With this understanding, Viktor saw that disillusionments following Chernobyl and the war in Afghanistan, a loss of confidence in the Party, and a collapsing economy were symptoms of a fractured Soviet society. He knew these led to Ukraine's separation from the Soviet Union and, in 1991, its independence (Chapter 17). At life's end, he also knew that Communism had gone wrong. But still questions remained. His parents had believed, and had taught him by word and deed, that people should work together and share what they had. Were they wrong? Or was this idea some fundamental principle of a supreme intelligence that created the universe? Was Communism a good idea, just shamefully applied, or would it never work? While Viktor never found answers, he did find peace in the love of his family, and in the confidence that he had served his country well (Chapter 17).

This twentieth-century memoir is the story of the Kramchaninov family struggling with external events beyond their control within a society going from one crisis to another. Being intimately involved in so many of the century's events, this family may even be a microcosm of Soviet times. The story is an odyssey of faith, for Viktor in particular and perhaps even a universal one for humankind, where teachings of childhood contradict subsequent life experiences and the power of propaganda retains its hold even on the minds of those who have seen the truth. Somewhere within the dreams and realities of this family lies the true essence of the birth, life, and death of the Soviet Union.

The Editors

1

My Father Joined the Bolsheviks

Viktor Kramchaninov

For better times he waits throughout the centuries;
As yet he waits in vain,
Through years of ruin, and the Tartar's miseries,
And serfdom's yoke and pain.

—From *The Hireling* by Ivano Franko (1856-1916)[1]

א

Without the past there is no future. And, unfortunately, as time passes, the years erase human memory. When my grandsons and granddaughters grow up, they will someday want to know who their ancestors were, what their lives were like, and why my parents were attracted to socialism. So now I have resolved to tell something of our story. Although I cannot vouch for its literary value, I can vouch for its truth.

My family was from the village Ksenyevka, near Gorlovka, within the Donbass region. In this industrial region close to Russia, the coal deposits are very large. In my village, half of the men worked in industry, either in the mines or in manufacturing, while the other half farmed the land. To make a living, my ancestors would have needed to work both on the land and in industry.

1 Published in English translation by Andrusyshen and Kirkconnell (1963, p204).

My grandfather, Arhip, had a large garden. He also mined coal, leading the horses that hauled wagons from the coalface to the lift. The horses had been brought into the mine while still young and, having lived underground without seeing the sun, they became blind. In order to hurry them along in their work, they had to be led. Later, Arhip worked at the coalface with a pick and shovel. During the war of 1877-1878 between Russia and Turkey, he served in the army on the Caucasian front. After the war was over, he brought home a wife, a young Georgian girl named Natalia, who became my grandmother.

Natalia did not understand Ukrainian, and so for a long time she hardly spoke, but she gave birth to eleven children and lived to the age of a hundred and five. In the 1960s, when I was in Gorlovka and saw her for the last time, she was a dried-up, gray-haired, crooked little old woman. Though she moved slowly, she kept house all by herself, could thread a needle without glasses, and maintained her independent spirit. That day, as she was sitting quietly on a small homemade bench in the middle of a courtyard, Aleksey, her three-year-old great-grandson, was running around in every direction, pushing his toy pram. The pram rolled into my grandmother and stopped.

Aleksey shouted, "Well, move, you old woman!"

And Grandmother replied, "Why, you little son-of-a-bitch, I will spank your ass with this birch rod."

"But," said Aleksey, "you cannot catch me!"

At first, I roared with laughter to hear such banter across the generations. But then I stopped, for I realized that my grandmother's life had not been easy. She had raised all those children, with so little money, through turbulent times. "One expects no respect from a boy of only three summers," I thought, "but she deserves all the respect that I can give her." She had never been educated and could neither read nor write, but she had sent my father, Panteley, to school. She and Arhip struggled for every *kopeck*, but they gave him property when he married. In his turn, Panteley made sure I was educated and, without that, I would not have had my aeronautical career. Generations build on the generations before, and Natalia had done her part to help me succeed.

Of Natalia's eleven children, nine were boys. Of the two girls, Uliana and Olga, I knew Aunt Olga better. In 1982, when visiting Donbass, I went to see her in her village close to Gorlovka. Even though she had become old, I found to my great pleasure that she was the same kind and beautiful person I had known in my youth. When she saw me, she began to cry. Knowing my plane soon left for Kiev, she began to fret about what she could give me to remember this day. As we were walking out through her front garden, where her three cherry trees stood, she suddenly asked me to take a bucket of cherries with me on the plane. She quickly found a stool and, standing on it, began to pick the cherries. But I soon saw I had to help her, for tears clouded her eyes, and her palsied hands, shaking with age and excitement, could hardly pick the fruit. We had not seen each other for forty years, yet we knew each other as though it were yesterday.

My recollections of my uncles and my other aunt are very vague. Uncle Ivan, the eldest, died before the Great Patriotic War[2], leaving his wife, Aunt Anastasia, and three children. In 1942, Uncle Nikolai died in Leningrad, defending his city in that fierce battle. He left a daughter, Ludmila, who was then brought up in a children's home. After the war, she went to school in Leningrad and became a teacher. In the forty years since, I have received only one letter, which said that she was satisfied with life as a teacher in Kamchatka, the large volcanic peninsula projecting into the Pacific Ocean close to the Aleutian Islands, thousands of miles to the east.

My father, Panteley Kramchaninov, born in 1895, and my mother, Barbara Tsapa, born in 1896, were married in 1914. In a yellowed and treasured photograph from that year, they stand together so young and beautiful. Father, a large lock of hair across his forehead, is handsomely dressed in a white shirt, a vest, and black

2 The "Great Patriotic War" is what Russia and the other former Socialist Republics call World War II.

trousers tucked into high boots. Mother, with her slender waist, is dressed in a bridal gown and wears a white bridal veil, as was the custom for Cossack women of the Donbass.

Wedding photograph from 1914 of Viktor's parents, Panteley Kramchaninov and Barbara Tsapa.

My mother's parents were peasants. They also lived in Father's village of Ksenyevka, and while some of the Cossacks there spoke Russian, her family spoke Ukrainian. I never knew her father, Timofey Tsapa, for he drank himself into an early grave. While he lived, he worked as a peasant, plowing the land. In the only photograph I ever saw, he was in the traditional Astrakhan cap and wore a beard. Of his many siblings, I can remember well only two of the sisters and three brothers. They were all peasants and, after the October Revolution of 1917, the brothers worked as laborers in the mines near Gorlovka. It was cheerless, dark, heavy work. When payday came, their wives were first in line at the paymaster's window, to collect the salaries so that my great-uncles couldn't drink up all the money at the local tavern.

The Tsapa family circa 1913. Seated: Yefosina and Timofey (wearing an Astrakhan fur cap) Tsapa, Barbara's parents. Standing: from left, Barbara, age seventeen, and her sister, Stepanida. Barbara became Viktor Kramchaninov's mother.

Within a year of my parents' marriage, Grandfather Arhip divided his property to give them a dessiatin (2.75 acres) of land and a heifer. On the edge of the village, close to an active railroad, the young couple built for themselves a small cottage with a thatched roof. During the mobilization for World War I, Father was not quite twenty years of age and was not conscripted. He worked in the coal mine with a pick and shovel. By 1918, civil war was raging. Young men were forced into whichever "volunteer" army happened to be controlling the Donbass region. Usually, this was the army of the anarchist, Makhno, or that of the White Guard under Denikin. Father had been able to escape "volunteering."

When Budjonny's Horse Cavalry of the Red Army was occupying the Donbass, a sailor from Petrograd (formerly St. Petersburg) encouraged Father to join the Bolsheviks. Father could read and write, he knew farming, coal mining, and he could repair anything that was broken, but he knew little of politics. It was a confusing time, because there were many political parties, each touting its own program. The sailor was confident, enthusiastic, and persuasive. He told Father about the Revolution: how the Bolsheviks took over the government in Petrograd, and how they promised that land would no longer belong only to the rich, but would be divided among all the people. Everyone would work together and all would have enough bread. He painted the rosy picture of how the poor would benefit from the socialist system. It was an attractive future to Father, whose parents and grandparents had to work so hard just to eat. For his own family to survive, Father had to farm his plot of land himself, as well as mine coal. Without some new policy, this hard life would continue for generations to come. Eager to break the pattern that had bound his ancestors, Father accepted the sailor's picture, and to help bring in the change, he joined the Bolshevik army.

Not long after Father volunteered, the Bolsheviks were victorious in the Civil War, and he was released from the army without going into combat. It was in his village of Ksenyevka that six of his children were born: Natalia (1916), Katerina (1918), Nikolai (1920), myself (1922), Alexander (1924), and Gregory (1928). To support his growing family, Father had returned to farming his dessiatin of land and to working in the coal mine. Adding to that the commute from our village to the mine in Gorlovka, he had no free time. Mother was not idle either. In addition to caring for us children and the house, she fed and milked the cow, helped Father in our garden, and preserved the vegetables for the winter. This effort did not bring prosperity, but it did bring survival. Others were less fortunate in those hard years after the revolution and many died of disease or starvation. Still, my parents held to the vision that the Petrograd sailor had described to Father. If all people were equal, worked together, and shared what they had, surely a better life would come. It would only be a matter of time. My parents were among those sustained by hope and anticipation. Their optimism flowed to us children and we adopted it. Later, when I was fighting in the Great Patriotic War, this hope even led me to become a member of the Communist Party. I have never doubted that people should work together and help each other. But to tell the truth, as I grew older, I began to doubt that Party leaders could make it happen.

Viktor P. Kramchaninov

2

My Boyhood on a Collective Farm

Viktor Kramchaninov

Aeneas was a lively fellow,
Lusty as any Cossack blade,
In every kind of mischief mellow,
The staunchest tramp to ply his trade.

—From *Travesty on Virgil's Aeneid*
by Ivan Kotliarevsky (1769-1838)[3]

א

How well I remember our thatch-roofed cottage in the village of Ksenyevka where I spent the first seven years of my life. There was the grass-covered yard and the kitchen garden, watered by a broad spring, which flowed from under the railroad embankment. Of my early childhood memories, one of the most vivid is of gypsies. During the 1920s, groups of them frequently roamed from place to place in the Donbass region and, as we lived on the edge of the village, they camped near our house. Their presence filled me with fear. Barely had they set up their tents, when many barefooted, noisy and

3 Published in English translation by Andrusyshen and Kirkconnell (1963, p37). Viktor liked this poem so much that he memorized extensive passages. Written in the vernacular of the common Ukrainian, the poem is a near-burlesque, where Virgil's Trojans become Ukrainian Cossacks, and oppressive Olympian gods become ruthless landlords.

active children emerged and began to unharness the horses. Within half an hour a blacksmith's forge was already hot, and the sound of hammers on the anvil could be heard as the gypsy men made horseshoes, wheels, and pokers to exchange for bread, vegetables, eggs, and bacon. Soon, gypsy women were walking among the houses persuading the housewives to have their fortunes told with cards in exchange for whatever household items they could provide, or even a kerchief or old shoes. We have a saying: "Some ask for bread, some for salt, and some for a piece of lard"—the gypsies were eager for anything.

Along with the young gypsy women were an amazing number of children. They would distract the housewife and, without fail, steal something from her. Whatever they took they hid at once among the folds of the very wide gypsy skirts, where discovery was impossible. When we children were disobedient, my mother, Barbara, would threaten to give us to the gypsies, which would immediately make us behave, for we were afraid of them.

The young gypsy boys and girls sang so very well that they entertained at weddings, performing their fiery dancing accompanied by the tambourine. And for five *kopecks* a gypsy boy would "dance on his belly," where he would lie face down, protrude his abdomen and, holding his hands and feet off the ground, bounce up and down on his belly, while at the same time spinning around like a top. It was remarkable. I remember one day when a gypsy man with a black mustache and a large horsewhip came into our yard to bargain for hay. In exchange for two horseshoes, my father, Panteley, agreed that he could have as much hay as he could carry "on his whip." So skillfully did he employ his whip and secure hay to it that he could not lift the hay to his shoulders and he had to ask Father for help. After Father had helped him lift the load, we children were amazed to see a stack of hay staggering out of the yard with nothing visible beneath it but two wobbly legs.

In those years my parents' possessions consisted entirely of their house, the garden, a horse and a cow, their dessiatin[4] of land, and a shed where the cart and plow were kept and where the hay was stored. At that time peasants were classified as either poor, average, or rich. As we were neither rich, nor poor, I suppose we fell into the average class, which turned out to be lucky for us.

In 1929, Stalin began the collective farms and we were swept up into it. We were among the "twenty thousand," the vanguard of millions of transplanted Ukrainians. We were required to move and leave everything behind: our land, house, animals, implements, and Father's job in the mine. But we were among the more fortunate, because Father was assigned to be a manager. The assignment probably came because he was not wealthy and he had volunteered for the Bolsheviks, but he was also well liked, and could read and write. We were sent to a farm called Veseliy, which means cheerful. The name came from the cheerful whistling sounds made by a huge, gnarled three-hundred-year-old oak when the wind blew, which in the Donbass was most of the time. It was on land that had belonged to a rich landowner named Kotliarevsky, and I never knew what happened to him. The farm was renamed "Progress" and Father remained chairman of it until 1933.

Kotliarevsky had been wealthy. His family had lived in a large house with four columns at the front. Not only the house, but also the stables and barns were built of red brick, a sign of prosperity. Red brick houses and farm buildings were unusual in eastern Ukraine where the peasants used only yellow bricks, which they could make themselves. Kotliarevsky had machinery: plows, harrows, and seeders. His house stood majestically on a high hill. Just behind the house there was a garden, which descended into a lovely wood, from which a path led down to a pond. Near the house stood a large, deep well, topped by a sturdy wooden frame. On the slopes below, there were ten thatched cottages and, in the distance, one could see

4 Desiaina (tithing) is an old Russian unit of land area, or about 1 hectare or 2.5 acres

villages and the neighboring Brodsky Farm. The countryside was all very beautiful. I passed a barefooted and happy childhood there. Looking back, I note with irony that Kotliarevsky shared a name with one of my favorite poets, but I never knew if they were related.

With Father being farm chairman, our family, for the first time, lived in a landowner's house. After we had lived there for about a year, the house mysteriously burned. None of us was hurt, but we lost all our possessions. Arson was rumored, and though no one was ever accused, it was likely. Maybe living in a fine house disguised our poverty, and resentment existed that someone lived more comfortably than everyone else. Furthermore, families resented being uprooted, losing their land and livestock, and being forced to move to the collective farms. People took their anger out on local Party officials and on farm directors. Arson or not, after the fire, our family was treated kindly by the farm workers. Everyone joined together willingly and in good humor to build us a new house by the *toloka* method, which means the whole settlement worked as one. The men rolled up their trousers above the knees, the women tucked up their skirts, and we all cheerfully kneaded clay with straw, then pushed it into the wooden rectangular forms. After the forms were removed, the familiar yellow bricks were sun dried for some days, and were then used for the walls.

For those times, it was rather a big house. There was a large drawing room, a room for the children, a kitchen, a storeroom and, under the same roof, sheds for coal, firewood, hay, and even for the cow. For our family, the village council allocated one hectare (about 2.5 acres) of ground, to include the yard and the garden. It was enough, because produce from the garden and milk from the cow fed all the family. Father worked from sunrise to sunset. Mother prepared the food, baked the bread, did the washing, made all our clothes, and kept the house. And we children did the gardening and gathered forage for the cow. I have marveled that our family worked so hard and in harmony at our different tasks, almost like chamber musicians, who play by memory on different instruments. During the day Mother led, mostly by example, occasionally by exhortation, and rarely by punishment. When Father came home, he took undisputed command. Being two such strong people, my parents must have had differences of opinion, but they were hidden from us children.

I well remember the necessity for hard work in the garden. In spring, we worked for days to prepare our large garden, using a spade to turn the dirt. Then we planted the potatoes, corn, string beans, beets, tomatoes, cucumbers, cabbage, and other vegetables. To eliminate the weeds, we hoed the whole garden at least three times each summer. Though the Donbass soil is wonderfully fertile and black, there are frequent droughts. When a dry wind blows from the Caspian steppes and when, in the summer months, there is not even one small cloud in the sky, a garden can quickly come to naught. To save it, we children watered our entire garden by night, plant by plant. Using buckets, we carried water from the pond up the steepest part of the path to our cart, on which we had set a barrel. Then, Nikolai and I were yoked like oxen to the cart. With us pulling, and with Natalia and Katerina pushing from behind, we hauled the cart and barrel up a gentler slope through the wood for half a mile to the garden. If we were inferior to oxen in strength, we compensated by the care with which we dispensed the water. With a quart-sized tankard, we measured the life-giving fluid for each plant. For dry days, we hauled at least five barrels. In those summers when there was some rain, the work was easier. In autumn, the vegetables were harvested and stored for the winter. We made sure our garden always yielded a good crop. We couldn't relax, but we were proud to be feeding our family. Early in life we learned the value of hard work, for without it we would starve. We believed our parents when they said, "Whoever relies on someone else for his soup, will keep his hunger for a long time."

One autumn, after the house had been built, Father brought home fruit tree saplings, which we planted in the garden. While we watered them to make them grow as fast as possible, we boys were too impatient to wait for them to bear fruit, and so from time to time we helped ourselves to apples and pears from other gardens. When the watermelons and muskmelons ripened, we made raids in the fields. Each of us would grab two melons and then run to hide in the tall corn. After breaking a melon in half over our knees, we enjoyed these gifts of nature by thrusting our faces deep into the fragrant pulp. Of course, with dust from the fields having stuck to our wet faces, our mother did not need ask where we had been—one glance and all was clear. To tell the truth, such raids on the melon farm were not taken very seriously, for if the watchman caught us he would only tweak our ears. But to catch us was extremely difficult, for we could run much faster than he.

Father and Mother wanted all of us children to be educated. While Father had attended school for four winters, Mother had not gone at all, for in her day rural people asked, "Why does a girl need education?" I never knew the source of her drive to learn, but she rebelled against the rural stereotype, probably because she saw a new era, and a new broom sweeps in a new way. She was not afraid to sweep with this new broom. In 1929, when she already had six children, she responded to the government's posters that "guarantee[d] the decision of the Party to eliminate illiteracy." She enrolled in the program and learned to read and write. She and Father wanted more for their children, both boys and girls, than they had been given. I believe they instinctively knew that education was the way out of poverty. In those days, elementary schooling was not compulsory, but was available at the request of the family. So in 1930, when I was seven, Mother enrolled me in a nearby one-room school in Alexandrovka. There being four classes of students, but only one teacher, she staggered the schedule. In the mornings, the first and second grades met together and, in the afternoon, the third and fourth grades met. Fortunately, the room was large enough to hold four rows of desks, one row for the ten to fifteen students in each grade. Because every student had a desk, all four grades could occasionally meet together.

Our teacher, Natalia Fedorovna, was quite old, but we loved her so much that we were very obedient. In the first grade, we learned the alphabet and, in order to write our letters well, we frequently practiced our strokes and circles. Drawing was studied in the second year, arithmetic in the third, and reading and science in the fourth. I was so eager to learn, and so much enjoyed studying science with the teacher, that the idea of playing hooky never entered my mind. The school was more than a mile from home. As we were very poor and had almost no money for clothes or shoes, we walked to school barefoot right up until the snow. In the winter when the ground was white, Nikolai, two years older than myself, and I took turns going to school, because we had only one pair of *valenki* felt boots. He would wear them to school one day, and I the next. On those days when he wore the boots, he would bring back my homework assignments, and on my days I would do the same for him.

I experienced one unpleasant incident at school. When I was in the fourth grade, our teacher told me I was the best student, and would receive as a prize a pair of new boots! As was customary, the award ceremony was to take place in the council house of a nearby village, Nikolaevka, and would be held on 7 November, the holiday for celebrating the October Revolution. All the children and the teacher would walk from the school to Nikolaevka with our banner, which we would display before the council. As usual, before the prizes were awarded, the chairman would make a speech about the Revolution, the brass band would play the Internationale, and everyone would sing. But one should only count chickens when the eggs have hatched. Unfortunately, on the day of the celebration, a heavy snow had fallen overnight and it was Nikolai's turn to wear our boots. Unable to walk barefooted to school and to the ceremony through the deep snow, I remained at home. But instead of giving the prize boots to Nikolai for me, they made the award to the second best student, a girl named Nina Chala. I felt this loss for a very long time because, if I had been given the boots, I could have gone to school every day.

But there were still times of good fun. One winter, using a knife, I carved a triangular-shaped ice skate from a block of wood, and using a hot nail, I bored a hole in the front and in the back. For a runner on the bottom of the skate, I used a length of heavy wire, which I made fast by drawing the ends up through the holes that I had bored. To attach the skate to the boot, I had two cords which I could tighten by twisting them with a small stick. The fit was about as good as a saddle on a cow but, with practice, I could manage rather well with this one homemade skate. On the way to and from school, we passed by a pond, and I must have cut a dashing figure skating in circles on one foot. When I wanted to show off, I would skate very fast over thin ice, which made cracking noises under my foot. How well I remember the time the ice broke and I fell in. I did manage to get out, but when I got home, all of my clothes were frozen stiff. Mother cried out, "What in the devil have you done?" She got me out of those frozen clothes, and promptly gave me a spanking. But then she gave me some hot linden blossom tea, put me near the fire, and dried my clothes on the furnace. I didn't catch cold or even sneeze once. Maybe bathing in the pond through the autumn and going barefoot until winter had conditioned me to the cold.

Our government would not allow celebration at Christmas, but my parents always organized one on New Year's Day. In our largest room, Father placed the biggest evergreen tree he could get into the house. All the children on the farm and those from the nearest villages were invited. After everyone helped put the homemade decorations on the tree, there were games, songs, and performances. And of course, every child went away with a gift that Mother had made—a souvenir, candy, or a spice cake. It was a merry festival that all the children looked forward to each year. My parents were very popular because of it. They were sociable and always glad to share whatever they had. The good will toward them may have saved Father's life later, when he was charged in court before the local Soviet council. It also may have helped Mother get the restaurant job that kept us alive during the famine.

With the arrival of spring, life always became much brighter, for there were new things to do. The most fun was the "night watch," when we boys took the horses to their night pasture. On those evenings we lads rode the horses bareback, galloping three miles to a meadow behind the Brodsky Farm. There, with rope fetters hobbling their front legs, the horses grazed all night, while we went home on foot. In the morning we returned and, holding to the horses' manes, we galloped home. Because of all this galloping, the skin on my bottom became raw and my tailbone ached, but I wouldn't give up the galloping for anything. When, on occasion, we spent the night in the meadow, we kindled a fire from dry horse dung, sat around it in a circle and took turns telling horrible ghost stories. Surrounded by utter darkness, listening to the stories, we were not reassured even by the sound of the horses munching the grass, for when there was the hooting of an owl, or the rustle of mice, we huddled up with fear. Yet, somehow, sunrise always found us fast asleep curled up on the ground. I loved to bathe the horses also, by riding them into the pond and, while clutching the mane, swimming into the deep water. When we came out of the water, the horse would stand patiently while I brushed its coat. And even though I was a mere boy, it would instantly obey me and turn this way or that on command as I brushed.

In autumn, winter, and spring, we four brothers slept together on a wooden shelf built into one corner of the room. We had but one blanket, which we shared. With four boys in such close quarters, arguments could easily arise. If we began to fight for any reason, there were too many of us for Mother to find out who was guilty. To solve the problem, she would spank each of us in succession with a wet sack, and immediately the fighting would cease. Not only was it humiliating punishment, but we were afraid of the wet cloth more than of the belt. In the summer we usually slept outside in the yard in our wide sledge, which stood on two logs to prevent the runners from rusting. Hay piled deep served as our mattress, and sackcloth as our blankets. If it were necessary to hide ill-gotten apples or melons, the sledge was the perfect place. On starry nights, as we lay on our backs, we would look at the Milky Way and, feeling like small specks in a giant universe, we would begin to dream. Already, as a young boy, I had begun to be interested in the vastness of the sky. Those were wonderful years, and later, during the war, I would think of them.

Viktor P. Kramchaninov

3

We Survived the Famine

Viktor Kramchaninov

Darkness will pass away, your fetters you will shed, ...

From *The Hireling* by Ivan Franko (1856-1916)[5]

ℵ

In the years before World War II, those most difficult for our family were 1931-1933. During the summers, there were unprecedented droughts throughout the whole country. These, plus the actions of our government resulted in severe famine. In 1931, the famine began in Siberia, and spread to the Volga region, Kazakhstan, North Caucasus and Ukraine. In August 1932, the "law of five ears," as we called it, decreed that persons hoarding or taking grain, even from their own land, were to be sentenced to ten years in prison or to be shot. No exceptions would be made. Even mothers stealing grain for starving children were shot as "enemies of the state." Many people died as a result of this law, and even more died of starvation. Directors of collective farms who allowed peasants to keep grain were denounced as saboteurs and either shot or given prison terms. Soviet brigades searched the houses and confiscated any food that

5 Published in English translation by Andrusyshen and Kirkconnell (1963, p204).

was found, with no consideration of children or pregnant women. Sometimes food that was collected rotted before it could be transported. By autumn of 1932, many peasants had migrated to the cities in search of work, leaving the harvest, poor as it was, ungathered.

In this time of emergency, Father happened to anger the Party. If a man knows where he will fall, he will spread straw, but Father suspected nothing. The farm's pedigree bull had broken its leg and became useless for breeding. Father authorized the slaughter of this bull to prevent starvation and afford the workers the strength to do the spring plowing and planting. Although people were fed, the Party was not impressed. Father had either failed to obtain permission from the chairman of the local Party cell, or he had done so improperly. He was formally accused of slaughtering livestock without permission. He could have been charged as an enemy of the state and been shot. But in the written accusation against Father, the local chairman of the Party presented to the court the lesser charge of "squandering socialist property." The Party was interested in political policy, not starving workers. Father had worked hard managing Progress Farm and he felt he had done a good job: the workers liked him. His reward was a sentence of three years in prison with hard labor. Our proverb, "I gave you all my rye, and yet you beat me," had come true.

One night, when two men from the secret police came to take Father away, I remember Mother screaming wildly at them, "What I shall do here alone with six children? How shall I feed them?" And indeed, days of great hunger followed. The food shortage soon became so severe that rationing began. Although Father served his sentence by helping construct an alabaster factory in Artemovsk not far away, he could not help us at all.

Mother was not one to give up; for her that was the ultimate weakness. She had a different philosophy: "Rely on God, but be careful not to make your own mistakes." In order to get a card for a scant pound of bread daily, one had to be a worker, while dependents only got half a pound. To qualify herself as a worker and get the greater food ration, Mother began to clean offices. With a pound of bread, one could just survive, but with the lesser ration, it was impossible. Mother was able to get an evening job in a restaurant where food for Party bosses was plentiful. She washed floors for no salary. Instead, she was given the leftovers, such as soup, cucumbers, and other vegetables. These, she brought home all mixed together in a bucket as unappetizing slop, but when there are no fish, even a crawfish is a fish. So whatever was in that bucket, we were grateful for, because otherwise we would have starved. We were so hungry that we consumed anything that was edible. In the early spring, we even ate young leaves of linden, nettle, and sorrel, but they did not satisfy us. We were too weak to attend school.

Eating whatever we could find had at least one unpleasant consequence. During the planting season, when we saw some barley remaining in the seeder, Nikolai and I ate the raw grain, hulls and all. Being indigestible, these hulls caused an impaction, completely blocking the outlet of the large bowel. We were in agony. When Mother laid Nikolai on his side to examine the problem, she found part of the impaction, as hard as stone, sticking out. Using a nail, and ignoring Nikolai's screams, she was able to pick apart the obstructing mass. Seeing Nikolai's suffering, I determined to avoid such torture. By huge effort, which threatened to push my eyeballs from their sockets, I evacuated an "egg" as large as a lamb and as hard as a rock.

Fortunately, the spring of 1933 came warm and wet. In order to have something to plant, we had scrupulously saved the eyes from uncooked potato skins which Mother had carried home in her bucket. Then, in the autumn, when the garden brought in a good harvest, we knew we had beaten the famine. We became strong again and returned to school. Later, when the construction of the alabaster factory was complete, Father was released from prison a year and a half early because of his exemplary work. He could no longer be employed on the farm, but he found a job in Chasov-Yar, four miles west of Artemovsk, where he did motor vehicle repair, for which he had a special talent. His earnings bought food and clothes. Our heifer gave birth to a female calf which we named "Dawn." Not only did her arrival increase our income, but also she was a young animal for us children to love. When she was weaned, our daily delight was to bring her a bag of grass which we ourselves had mown using a sickle. We also brought corn stalks and enough extra grass to provide forage for the winter. In Red Village, three miles away, there was a large park with many linden trees. When the trees were in bloom, Mother had all of us children bring home at least one bag of blossoms. These we dried and mixed with cherry twigs to make a very pleasant tea. Our lives began to be cheerful once more.

When I was in the fifth grade, we boys saw a doctor for the first time. Having eaten something that was contaminated, all four of us became feverish and began to vomit uncontrollably. Frightened, Mother called the doctor, who pumped our stomachs with a magnesium solution. To relieve colic, he gave us (and I remember the smell to this day) "drops of the Danish king," a tincture of the oil of anise. Then he left, telling Mother that we would soon be well. Indeed, the vomiting ceased and we could eat again. Less serious illnesses, Mother treated. For winter colds or the flu, her favorite treatment was linden blossom tea, which contained a natural aspirin. Bruises and scratches were never worth her attention. I do not recall that my parents were ever ill. I believe that an inherently strong constitution has carried our family through many difficulties.

In the fifth and sixth grades, I went to school in Chasov-Yar. From the seventh to the ninth grades, I went to the school at Charmotte. Both schools were more than two miles from home, but we were so used to walking and running that we thought nothing of the distance. Because I loved to study and reveled in learning new things, I worked hard at school. It was never necessary for my parents to make sure I had done my homework. At Charmotte, our school taught mathematics, physics, and history with great skill. School was exhilarating; I was happy there, and developed a love of learning that never left me. I was lucky to find a small rural school with such an exacting approach to knowledge; sometimes even a blind chicken finds the corn.

I was twelve years old before I ever saw a radio. I had heard music only when someone played the accordion or *balalaika*, or when there was a gramophone.[6] Hearing music gave me so much pleasure that I wanted to buy a *balalaika* and learn to play it myself. By collecting bottles, and selling them at a market six miles from home, I was able to get enough five-*kopeck* coins within a year to buy an instrument. After a very jolly tractor operator named Saenko taught me how to play by ear, I learned to pick out many tunes for folk dancing. Some evenings, leaning against the riverbank, I would play while the girls and boys of our neighborhood danced barefooted. After learning the *balalaika*, I learned to play by ear both the mandolin and the guitar. When the holidays came, I would bring the school instruments home to teach my brothers, Nikolai and Alexander. During these sessions, if they didn't play correctly, I would rap their knuckles. Even though this made them angry, they put up with my rough discipline—"Suffer a Cossack and you will become a General"—and they learned to play, and even bought their own instruments.

My ability to play musical instruments led me into music and theater at school. Our theatrical director was an enthusiastic young woman, the teacher of literature, who taught us to love our literary heritage. When we performed Pushkin's *Boris Godunov*, I learned the entire play by heart. In addition to other roles, I played the monk, Father Misail, in the act entitled "The Tavern on the Lithuanian Frontier." This was one of our school's evening performances, attended by our parents and the public. While walking the two miles to school and back, I memorized many writings by Pushkin, especially *Onegin's Journey* and *The Bronze Horseman*. I also learned by heart plays, prose and poetry by other authors. I especially loved the poems of our Ukrainian Shevchenko.

Gain knowledge, brothers! Think and read,
And to your neighbors' gifts pay heed,—
Yet do not thus neglect your own:
For he who is forgetful shown

6 The *balalaika* is a usually three-stringed instrument of Russian origin with a triangular body played by plucking or strumming.

Of his own mother, graceless elf,
Is punished by our God himself.

Blest be your children in these lands
By touch of your toil-hardened hands
And duly washed, kissed let them be
With lips that speak of liberty!
Then all the shame of days of old,
Forgotten, shall no more be told;
Then shall our day of hope arrive
Ukrainian glory shall revive.[7]

In addition to Pushkin and Shevchenko, I loved our other poets, including Franko, Lermontov, Kotliarevsky, and Nekrasov. I memorized many verses from these and other poets. Years later, during the war, when on night duty in the forest, or behind enemy lines with the partisans, I found that reciting the passages I had memorized was strangely comforting.

At home near the end of our garden was a ravine. At the bottom was a creek, which was usually dry but which flooded with muddy water during the spring rains. Father was ever inventive, and he noted that the ravine had a narrow outlet, suitable for a dam. He had a truck bring in large stones from the quarry, oak logs and a lot of brushwood. Using the logs as pilings, bracing them with the stones, and weaving in the brush, we built a dam about three feet high. The next spring, the rain created a small lake for us. When the lake drained, new soil had settled on this previously unusable ground. Now we had about an eighth of an acre of new garden, where we planted pumpkins, beets, tomatoes, and cabbage. We had never seen such a garden! Tomatoes weighed a pound each, pumpkins were three feet in diameter, and one beet grew to thirty-

7 Published in English translation from Shevchenko's *The Epistle* by Andrusyshen and Kirkconnell (1963, p135).

five pounds! Simply carrying such produce out of the ravine to the storage shed was heavy work.

My voice was getting deeper, I began to notice girls, and I wanted to look better. I had always worn homemade trousers, shirts and jackets made by Mother with her Singer sewing machine, but when I was fourteen, she bought me a cotton suit for the first time. I was sure that longer hair would be more appealing than the crew cut that my father gave me with his electric shears. Finally, when I was fifteen, he agreed to let my hair grow. It grew longer, but it wouldn't behave. It only stood straight up, and my comb was useless. Even when my hair was wet, it wouldn't lie down. I looked worse than when I had a crew cut. So I consulted my friend Saenko, the jolly tractor operator, and he advised me to use a cheap industrial grease. It made my hair lie down, but soon my scalp began to burn. Ashamed to go home with this problem, I ran to the pond and shampooed with wet clay. The grease came out, but my scalp began to peel the next day.

Barbara, age ninety-nine, in 1995,
while living with her daughter, Nina Drugov in L'viv.

During the summer vacations from the seventh grade on, I was old enough to drive harvesters and mowing machines on the collective farm. In the autumn, when I proudly brought home my earnings—bags of wheat, corn, millet, and sunflower seeds—my mother gave me high praise. I had worked before in our garden to help feed the family, and now, in these good years before the war, I found special pleasure in using the farm machinery to earn food.

On the farm was a popular young man named Nikolai Skotar, whom we all liked. He began to court my older sister Natalia and, in my opinion, she was not indifferent to his attention. When she graduated from high school, Natalia went to nursing school in Artemovsk. Two years later Katerina went to the teacher's college also in Artemovsk. In autumn, I would go there by train to bring them a basket of food from home. When Natalia finished nursing school, the government sent her to Gorlovka, where she was to be a nurse for the miners. There, a very glib reveler named Egor Bulgakov used smooth talk to persuade her to marry him, barely one month after they had met. He came "with portfolio"—that is, from an educated and wealthy family—and, despite his drinking, this "portfolio" impressed Natalia. When the two of them came to our parents for permission to wed, Father did not at all like this turn of events. Being an abrupt man, he roared at Natalia, "For some years now, Nikolai has courted you, but now after an acquaintance of only one month, you want to marry another man! Before jumping into hell, you should listen to your father." But Natalia did not listen. Unfortunately, Father's curt words made her angry and she became only more determined to go through with the marriage.

Natalia got her wish. All the family began to prepare for the wedding and to invite the guests. On the appointed morning, the couple went to the magistrate and registered their marriage but, in the evening, when the ceremony was to have occurred, the bride had disappeared! Nikolai had called on Natalia asking her to marry him. And she, bridal veil and all, had gone with him! They were gone the whole night. When she returned in the morning, she announced that she loved Nikolai and would marry him rather than Egor.

Father was a stern disciplinarian—a law unto himself. He angrily declared, "You should have thought of this earlier!" His authority and the honor of the family had been violated. What happened next was not entirely known to the family or guests, but Father took Natalia to the shed. When they emerged she had welts that a belt could have made. The wedding proceeded as planned, hitching a beaten doe and a wild stallion to the same wagon. Natalia, welts and all, left with Egor to live in Gorlovka. After she married Egor, Natalia couldn't wash a black dog white. As time passed, he drank more and more and worked less and less, and Natalia became resigned to her fate. She had four children, three girls and a boy, and, despite Egor's drunkenness, all of them turned out well, became educated and then married. Throughout her life with Egor, Natalia suffered, and near the end, when she became ill, she left him and went to live with a daughter, where she died. Hot blood and impetuous action are costly, and Natalia had paid the price.

I often wondered if Father had been too severe with Natalia at this crucial point in her life, but our family was defined by discipline. For generations, we were practical country people. The wisdom of our ancestors came not from books, but through experience, and hard work ensured their survival. Our parents were no exception. They arose early each morning, and never neglected the day's tasks. Whatever the obstacle, they were equal to it. They, like the generations before them, maintained strict discipline, so that the children could distinguish right from wrong. At an unfortunate moment, Natalia had challenged traditional parental authority.

I remember in particular how my mother worked so hard without complaining. She could do nearly everything skillfully, canning the fruits and vegetables, making the clothes, and even repairing the furnace. When she became old, she went to live in L'viv with her youngest daughter, Nina Kramchaninova-Drugova. Even though it was no longer necessary for her to work so hard, she still made all her own clothes, sewed for the family, and helped with the cooking, shopping, and cleaning. So much changed in her world while she was raising her own children, helping with the grandchildren, and looking after ten great-grandchildren. She went through the Revolution, occupation by marauding armies, depressions, famines, collectivization of the farms and two wars, yet even at ninety-nine years old, she did not worry about her advancing age, and she still enjoyed a glass of vodka on holidays. A busy life of continuous labor had actually helped her to retain her vivacity. A determined Slavic mother, one of nature's strongest forces, got us through the famine of 1931-33.

As I look back, I remember that Ukrainians could not even mention The Great Famine beyond the family. The subject was taboo. Only since Gorbachev's *perestroika* in the 1980s have we been able to discuss it. Officials have said that despite poor harvests, Stalin had to sell grain to buy industrial equipment, and poor oversight led to excessive force. Even so, it is hard to understand why grain exports increased more and more while grain prices were falling sharply. Whatever was the cause of this famine, many died and our family barely survived.

Viktor P. Kramchaninov

4

The Years Before the War

Viktor Kramchaninov

On heaven's ethereal ocean,
rudderless and without sail,
starry choirs in ordered motion
calmly float through vapor's veil ...

From *The Demon* by Mikhail Lermontov (1814-1841)[8]

א

In 1939, the pace of change accelerated. Stalin was intent on a faster industrialization of the Soviet Union. In Ukraine we had a shortage of skilled labor, and finding men who could maintain and repair motor vehicles became a national priority. Because he was an expert mechanic, my father was sent by the government to be a consultant to the Stalin Factory in Zhitomyr, about seventy miles due west of Kiev. The fact that Father had recently been imprisoned for "squandering socialist property" now seemed forgotten. The government sensed a coming emergency and experienced men were enlisted to meet the nation's needs, even if they had been exiled or imprisoned for various "crimes." Literally thousands of innocent people who were, or had recently been, imprisoned were suddenly available to work. Father was one of these.

8 Published in English translation by Charles Johnson (1983, p118).

I was seventeen when Father went to Zhitomyr, and I took time off from school to go with him for his first few days there. We rented lodgings in the house of an elderly Jew. Soon after Father began the job, a large industrial transport that had been damaged in an accident was towed into the factory. Since this truck was needed urgently for construction, the factory manager did not assign it to the queue of vehicles for routine repair. Instead, in an exceptional move for a Communist factory, he offered Father a lump sum to do the job. Now I saw firsthand how well Father worked. He enlisted my help and the help of two of his most competent co-workers. He showed us exactly what needed to be done and how best to do it. We worked nights and through the weekend until the job was done—done well, and in record time. The manager was impressed. Father received high praise and, remarkably for those days, a large cash payment.

It was cause for a celebration, which Father arranged at our lodgings. In the evening, we four and our Jewish host gathered around a table loaded with potatoes boiled in "kings' coats" (with the peel still on), sauerkraut, herrings, onions, and black bread. There was no shortage of vodka: three quarts were on the table. Father's comrades poured vodka into six-ounce glasses. The party began with the familiar Ukrainian congratulatory toast: "To Life and Health!" Our host must have believed the proverb "Vodka is healthy for Ukrainians, but deadly for Jews," for he drank no vodka and joined the toast with only a modest glass of wine. We all set upon the food. At that time, I did not drink vodka and, after eating all I wanted, I retired to the kitchen and to my homework assignments, which would be due when I returned to school. However, I could hear another toast and knew that Father and his friends had drained their glasses again. Our host did not join in, and suggested that the party was getting too boisterous. He urged his guests to drink less and to be quieter. There were more toasts. Worried, our host said that he was the owner of the house and, if the police came, he would be the one arrested. He wasted his breath, for the vodka had increased the appetites of his guests and lubricated their throats for song. For the whole evening he was beset with the most uncontrollable fear that the police would come, but the party was now beyond restraint. Fortunately, the police did not come and no unpleasant incident occurred. The next day, Father only needed a "freshening nip"—a small glass of vodka and a large glass of sauerkraut juice—to assuage his headache.

The factory manager now fully recognized Father's mechanical ability. After Father had been in Zhitomyr only a month, he was offered a permanent position, and he took it. On coming home, he presented the idea of a move to the other four members of the family—Mother, myself, Alexander and Gregory. By now, both Katerina and Natalia were married and living in the Donbass, and Nikolai was in his second year at the Economic Institute in Odessa. Father's salary was to be the same, but prices were lower in Zhitomyr than in the Donbass and life was better. Even the name, Zhitomyr, meaning "place of abundant rye," sounded good. Mother liked the idea of a new life, and we boys were excited at the prospect of going to another part of the country. So, in the summer of 1939, we five moved from our village in the Donbass to the city of Zhitomyr. After living temporarily in an apartment on Sokolov Mountain, we moved to a most pleasant house at 7 Korbutovka Street, near one of Europe's most beautiful rivers, the Teterev[9]. Across the river from our house was a stately forest of hardwoods and evergreens. Being near a beautiful river, I took up fishing, which I have loved ever since.

In the autumn of 1939 in Zhitomyr, I entered the tenth and final grade of high school. When I went to School Number 32, about two and a half miles from home, I was disappointed to find poor teachers in an old building with small rooms. After a few days, I left to go to School Number 36, five miles from home. Walking twice as far was worth the effort. The building was new, the rooms spacious and well-planned, and the teachers were young and enthusiastic. After the principal had introduced me to my class, telling them that I had

9 Teterev (Ukr. Teteriv) is a river in Ukraine, the right tributary of the Dnieper, and flows into the Kiev reservoir. In English, Teterev means "black grouse."

just arrived from Donbass, I was assigned to share a desk with a quiet girl, Maria Rudenko.[10] Although I did not know it then, Maria and I were destined to share much more than a desk.

Maria as a young woman, before her marriage, 1939.

In my poor cotton trousers and faded sateen shirt, I made a shabby appearance compared to the other students. Zhitomyr was a rather prosperous city, and the students here wore better and more fashionable clothes than in the Donbass. Also, because I was a new student from a small village, the teachers wondered if I could meet the academic standards of the school. For each subject in turn, they questioned me. The teacher of algebra and mathematics asked me to solve a problem, which I did in under two minutes. Then he gave me a more difficult geometry problem which concerned a rotat-

10 Maria remembers rather differently how Viktor was assigned to sit with her at the same desk (see chapter 5).

ing body. I drew the illustration on the board and pointed out that there were three ways to solve the problem. When I gave the answer, he congratulated me, even coming over to shake my hand. As all the other teachers were also pleased with my answers, the guys in the class saw that I was not just a country hick and they started to respect me. Soon I was elected as the class monitor and chairman of the student committee. I needn't have worried about my shabby clothes, because our beloved mathematics teacher had the nickname of "ragged-assed Europhile"; in addition to mathematics, he knew nearly everything about European history, literature and painting, but his trousers were baggy, ragged, and patched.

Our class was so congenial that we even came back to school in the evenings, to play our instruments and sing. Our school had an orchestra, directed by Viktor Spirin, a young teacher whom we guys liked very much and whom the girls idolized. He would join us on some of our musical evenings at the school. He encouraged us to look up at the sky and marvel at its vastness, its constellations, and its planets. On Progress Farm I had loved the night sky, and this was even better. Enthusiastic teachers and eager friends made learning easy and fun. Maria Rudenko, my desk companion, was also a good student. With her natural aptitude for languages and my mathematical abilities, we could help each other with our studies. I felt a growing attachment to this quiet girl with her enchanting smile and reddish-golden hair, but I was ashamed to let her know my feelings and I thought she could not guess them.

Air force officers sometimes came to our school from a nearby airbase to give special evening concerts. Musically, they were much better than we were, but our orchestra could play some classical music and sometimes we joined in. We enriched the evenings by reciting verses and singing songs. Maria was musical and had an excellent voice. After a concert, we usually went to the officers' club on the base, where there was a brass band and dancing—polkas, waltzes, and foxtrots. Our girls loved dancing with the officers, who were much better than we clumsy guys. Not surprisingly, after finishing school, some of the girls married the pilots who had been their dancing partners. It was because of these pleasant evenings, meeting these pilots, and dreaming of the vastness of the sky that I first began to think seriously of becoming a pilot myself.

With the coming of spring, this most pleasant school year drew to a close. We knew that preparation for our final examinations was serious business. A group of the guys would come to my house to study. We would wade across a nearby shallow stretch of the Teterev River to a clearing in the forest. There, taking each subject in its turn, the most knowledgeable student in the subject would lead discussions on the difficult points. Following study, and after spreading cloths on the ground, we shared whatever food we had brought. But alcohol was not allowed!

Although I enjoyed the sessions with the guys, I studied more often with Maria and her girlfriend, Raisa, in the forest clearing. Rolling up my trousers to cross the river, I would wade out carrying Maria and then Raisa in my arms, which I found most pleasantly exciting! As the days passed, I began to like Maria more and more, so it was hard to keep my mind on my studies. In the evenings, I began to call on her to go for walks in Central Park, and along the city streets. One evening we went to a movie where, unable to afford the better seats, we sat at the back. But sitting there, close to Maria and shyly holding her hand, I thought it was the best place on earth. I had no idea what was showing on the screen. One afternoon, on a high bluff overlooking the Teterev River, as we admired the beautiful view, I kissed Maria on the cheek. I was so happy and excited, I could easily have fallen down the cliff into the river.

We successfully passed our examinations in May 1940, and everyone—students, teachers, and parents—prepared for the graduation ceremony. For this solemn and sadly final occasion, tables were set up in the assembly hall, laid for the banquet and decorated with flowers. As the principal awarded the diploma to each graduating student, the school orchestra played a flourish and the audience applauded. In my case, it was graduation with high honors. Afterwards, there were speeches from the teachers and parents, with the usual kind words and good wishes, and responses from us, the students. These were followed by the banquet, amateur performances, and dancing until morning. Before the party ended, the whole class agreed to assemble a day later at my house for a picnic in the woods.

When the class arrived, all together and in high spirits, they burst into our yard. Mother greeted them warmly, and then unexpectedly asked of the girls:

"Which of you will be my daughter-in-law?"

Before any of them could recover, my brother Alexander shouted out:

"There she is—Maria Rudenko!"

This came as no surprise to anyone, including our family, for they had known Maria for months and had come to love her.

To get everyone across the river, we guys rolled up our trousers and carried the girls across in our arms. Once across, we ushered them to our clearing. As it was late in May, nature had kindly provided natural decoration with many wild flowers, including our favorite, lilies of the valley. There, surrounded by this fragrant beauty, we set up an improvised table and sat around it, eating and reminiscing about all the great and funny moments of our school year. It was one of the most splendid days of my life. We all decided to meet again in ten years' time. Later, when I was at the front, I would think of this day.

To my great sorrow, Maria and her family moved to L'viv to join her father after graduation. He had been sent there by our government to oversee construction work in what had been Poland, but was now western Ukraine. Maria entered the medical institute there, and we wrote to each other frequently, promising to visit. But it didn't happen. Unknown to us, the war was rapidly approaching. It would be five long years before we would see each other again.

Viktor P. Kramchaninov

5

My Girlhood in the Ukraine Republic

Maria Rudenko-Kramchaninova

Love your Ukraine, love as you would the sun,
The wind, the grasses and the streams together.
Love her in happy hours, when joys are won,
And love her in time of stormy weather.
Young woman! As you would her sky of blue,
Love her each moment that your days remain.
Your sweetheart will not keep his love for you,
Unless he knows you also love Ukraine.

From *Love Ukraine* by Volodimir Sosiura (1898-1965)[11]

א

My parents were Pavel and Christine Rudenko. The name Rudenko, which means red, came from my great-great-grandfather who had reddish-brown hair, which I inherited. I was born in 1922, when times were very hard. Near the end of the Civil War in 1920, my father, who had been fighting in Bessarabia with the Bolsheviks, returned home. There he found my grandfather, Moisey, but typhus, that scourge of war, had taken my grandmother. Father's sister and three brothers were still at home. Miraculously, their horse and cow had survived not only the war and its famines, but also the bandit raids. Having a horse, Grandfather and Father,

11 Published in English translation by Andrusyshen and Kirkconnell (1963, p423).

along with Father's two healthy brothers, were able to work their rich farmland near the village of Sotnykskoe in the Poltava Region. Father's epileptic brother could not do farm work, but helped his sister keep the house, do the cooking, and tend their kitchen garden.

Father could read and write, for he had had four years of education in a parish school before the Revolution. Even though he was not a Communist, his education and service in the Bolshevik army was enough for the Soviet authorities to nominate him as a member of the Village Council. For all practical purposes, the nomination ensured his election. In addition, he was cheerful, outgoing, and popular: not only could he play both the violin and the accordion, and sing well in a rich baritone, but he got along well with people and helped them solve their problems. Once elected, he soon organized a chorus and a theatrical troupe among the youth of the village. The Village Council had erected a hall where, on Sundays and holidays, the people were assembled for lectures on socialism, the rewards of Communism, and the harmfulness of religion. After the lectures, the choral and theatrical groups gave their performances, and their fame soon spread to the surrounding villages.

It was during a concert at the neighboring village of Majorcina, six miles away, that Father met Christine Popovich, and it was love at first sight. Although she was from a poor family, Christine was beautiful and had many prosperous suitors. Her parents urged her to marry into wealth and improve the family situation, but she had fallen in love with Pavel. They were married and went to live in his village where, in due course, two daughters—myself, and then Galina—were born.

Everyone was poor. As Village Council Chairman, Father was no better off than the rest for the job paid virtually no salary. To provide for his young family, he worked in nearby villages building houses and sheds. The grinding poverty of the peasants had cultivated seething resentment toward the new Bolshevik government during the Civil War years. Order was not possible, particularly in the rural areas. In acts of arson, known as "the red cock," homes of Party leaders and members of Village Councils were burned. Village leaders were even killed. One morning Father found a slip of paper in his front yard warning him of "the red cock." He understood only too well the risks to himself and his family. His neighbors and friends rallied round to guard his house day and night, but mother was afraid, and they decided to move their young family to the city of Lubni, where Father found construction work in a large factory.

There, Father excelled. He liked his job, performed it well, and was popular among his co-workers. To reward and encourage outstanding workers, the Soviet factory managers gave gifts as incentives, and Father was a frequent recipient. I remember the portrait of our Ukrainian poet, Taras Shevchenko, and the beautiful tea service decorated with light blue forget-me-not flowers. I kept one of the cups for a long time. In recognition of Father's abilities, the Soviet government sent him to a school for construction engineers. After graduating, he was assigned to a commune near the city of Mariupol, on the Sea of Azov, where he constructed buildings and animal pens. When he finished, we went with him to his next assignment in the village of Kustovtsi, near the western city of Khmelnitskiy.

We lived in a two-room apartment. There was a shed, and my parents were able to buy a cow and a pig. Galina and I went to school, Mother looked after the apartment and the animals, and, from sunrise to sunset, Father did construction on the farm. But he did not receive enough building materials, and those he was given were shoddy. Repeatedly, Father warned the Party of the coming winter and asked the Soviet managers for more and better material, but to no avail. When the winter came, it was very cold, and some of the farm animals died of exposure. It was the winter of 1932-33, when the Party severely punished farmers who slaughtered their animals. Someone had to be held responsible for any loss of livestock. The local Soviet council blamed Father, claiming sabotage. Such a charge was easy to sustain, for the Party taught that each person was a potential enemy of socialism. Father was arrested and sent to prison in the town of Polonnye.

Mother sold everything and we moved to be near Father. The famine had driven many people to leave Polonnye in search of survival. There were vacant apartments, and we moved into one of them. Mother had no job, and our meager savings were spent on a lawyer for Father. We lived on *kopecks*, yet twice weekly Mother took food to the prison because Father was near starvation. The winter continued bitterly cold, and we soon exhausted any coal that had been left in the shed. With no money to buy firewood, we burned whatever we could find. One day, when I was scraping coal dust from the ground in the shed, my hand hit something solid. Digging deeper, I found a hoard of silver coins! At that time there were special government shops that gave food in return for gold or silver. Mother took the coins, cleaned them till they shone, and exchanged them for flour, sugar and other foodstuffs. Our joy knew no bounds.

Father's case was brought to trial. Though the lawyer did what he could, Father was sentenced to three years of hard labor in the mines of southeastern Ukraine, in the town of Krivoy Rog. With us in tow, Mother returned to her own village, Majorcina, because she thought life would be easier there. But it wasn't.

The famine there in the Poltava Region was not because of a poor harvest, for it had been good. Rather, the wheat was taken from the people by brute force. The villagers were required to hand over their horses, cows, pigs, grain, and even potatoes to armed men who requisitioned food for the government. They took everything they could find, even the seed intended for spring planting. There was no consideration for children or pregnant women. Everyone who could move was required to go to work on the kolkhoz collective farms, where each person got half a pound of bread for each day's work. Children developed bloated bellies and died. We ate cattle food, acorns, beet tops, bran—whatever we could find. While we were starving, food was allowed to rot in the cellars of the collective farm. Potatoes froze in the fields. When we could get them, we thawed them, put the mash through a sieve, mixed it all with a little flour, and made patties which we baked. When spring came, life was a little easier. Fresh green nettle and linden leaves were dried, pounded into powder, mixed with flour, and baked into patties. They were green and crumbling, but they were edible.

Every day children with swollen bellies came to our house and asked for something to eat.[12] Often they would sing:

Father is in kolkhoz,
Mother is in kolkhoz,
Children sit by the road,
Bellies are naked, legs are bare,
But we accomplish the five-year plan!

There were "barbers"—women desperate to feed hungry children—who crept into the fields by night and used scissors to cut the heads of grain. During harvesting they secretly carried away grain hidden in pouches or in their bosoms. If caught by the guards, they were sent to prison or shot. Our family lived in this village for one year until Father, who had distinguished himself by his work, was released early from prison. He found a job as foreman on a kolkhoz in the Vinnitsa Region, not far from Zhitomyr, and our reunited family went with him. But we never forgot the horrors of the famine.

In 1936, Father was asked to build a school and kindergarten in the city of Zhitomyr. The city administration furnished us with an apartment near the building site. In the autumn of 1939, as soon as the school was finished, my class, for its tenth and final year of high school, were to move into the new building. For a few days before opening, my class worked all together to prepare the new building for the start of the school year. It was great fun, and we became the best of friends. We threw out the rubble left over from construction, washed the windows, and cleaned the floors.

During these days, I learned we were to have a new student join the class. While the school was being built, its director often

12 The plight of children in these years has been graphically described by Fitzpatrick (1999).

consulted with Father on the details of construction, and over the months they became close friends. It was the director who told me that a new student named Kramchaninov had arrived from the Donbass, and would join our class. The new student's father, he said, was an expert mechanic and had been assigned to the Stalin Factory. Well, how could I not tell this news to my classmates? While we worked, this new guy was the topic of conversation. Everyone wanted to know about him. Should we "pin" [13]him on the first day? This was a joke we played on dull-witted guys, who hadn't studied their physics and were ignorant about electricity; we would send them to the principal with an empty bucket to get it filled with "phase."[14] Since two students shared each desk, with whom would he sit? Everyone had a different opinion. The guys wanted to know if he played soccer and chess. The girls had other questions, but did not express them.

In September, students, parents, teachers, the school director, city and state authorities, heads of the trade unions, and journalists all assembled in the yard to dedicate the new building. The school director began by thanking the city and the Party. There were other speeches by the teachers, by the parents and even by the students. The mood was marvelous. Then the first bell rang to signal the start of classes. The younger students rushed inside, crowding through the door, but we, the more mature students, marched in a more dignified procession to our classroom on the second floor. We chose our places with care. Our teacher's desk had been covered with flowers. With a face as bright as the blossoms on her desk, our teacher, Rosalie Ruvimovna, thanked us for cleaning the building and welcomed us to our tenth and final academic year. Then she introduced the new student, Viktor Kramchaninov. Standing before us was a tall guy with an athletic build, and a confused smile on his face. The guys began vying with each other to invite him to

13 "Pin" means to make fun of or to laugh at someone.

14 Although a phase is an electricity concept, an unknowing student might believe it to be an actual substance, and would be sent to the principal's office with a bucket to obtain some "phase."

sit with them, but Viktor quickly chose Alex Podgora, a tall boy who was sitting at the back of the room. Alex and Viktor soon became fast friends and remained so for the rest of their lives.

For each subject we had a different teacher, who determined the new student's level of knowledge to ascertain if he was ready for the final year. Viktor performed at the highest level in each subject. When the school director, who taught mathematics, came in, he gave Viktor the most difficult problems, and Viktor solved them. The director was impressed and he shook Viktor's hand. Viktor's place in the class was established. Everyone liked this new guy, and after two weeks he was elected chairman of the student committee. So began our new and final academic year.

Still, guys are guys, and Alex and Viktor wrestled with each other in the back of the room. They called out the answers to questions, and argued out loud about them. This amused the other students, but it distracted the teachers. Finally, Alex and Viktor's games went too far. Our German teacher, a young woman, was leading the class. Our desks were arranged in three rows with wide aisles between each row. The desks were of an old design with a bench attached to a table, under which was a shelf for our books and papers. Alex and Viktor's long legs rested against the bottom of this shelf. When the teacher was writing on the board with her back to the class, Alex and Viktor, on half-bent legs, raised their desk with their knees. Looking as if they were still seated, they moved their desk down the aisle, while the whole class held its breath. They moved the desk behind the teacher and began to press her to the wall. She screamed and fell. The boys realized at once that they had gone too far and helped her to her feet, apologizing profusely, but enough is enough. The school principal came in and decided straightaway that such high-spirited guys must be separated. As I was the quietest one in the class, he assigned Viktor to sit at my desk.

Though the principal never said so aloud, it became my job to cultivate more tranquil behavior in Viktor. I never knew whether it was separation from Alex, some influence of mine, or the principal's reprimand, but the strategy worked, and Viktor caused no further disturbance. I never asked him whether he liked his new assignment, but I think both of us were secretly pleased, for we remained together amicably until the end of the academic year. We began to find pleasure in helping each other with our studies. Algebra and trigonometry did not come easily to me. For very hard problems, Viktor did not need to ask if I was having difficulty and would lead me through each step. During tests on mathematics, he silently worked on my problems first, and then his own, and was still the first to hand in his work to the teacher and to leave the room. My academic strengths lay in languages: German, Russian, and Ukrainian. When it was necessary, I silently helped Viktor in these subjects, but we never spoke of this—to each other or to anyone else.

I liked Viktor for his independence, his self-reliance, and his decency. He was a friend I could really depend on in any situation. Apparently, from the way we looked at each other, our classmates drew their own conclusions, even before we did. Of course, our class was at school during the day, but in the evenings we all gathered together to play in a string orchestra or to study the constellations with our astronomy teacher. On holidays, almost everyone would come to my house to dance to the gramophone. We were simply a group of young people who were all good friends; there were no cliques, and we did not divide up into couples.

However, Viktor and I began to realize that we were in love, although we were afraid to make a declaration of it even to ourselves. We denied our feelings until they were so strong we could no longer ignore them. Then came the spring, when all nature awoke, the green shoots appeared, and the air was filled with lilac. Viktor invited me to take a stroll with him in our wonderful park above the Teterev River. It is difficult to describe the tremor I felt as I waited for him to pick me up. On many previous occasions we had gone together to the city library to read something new and interesting, and to check out some books to take home, but these were related to our studies. We enjoyed talking about the usual everyday things, about events and our friends, but we never talked about our feelings. But that day, I felt like a different person. My heart beat rapidly, and

I counted each minute. I was ready long before he came. Viktor arrived on time; quiet, steady, and smiling. We went to our city park, full of flowers and young people. On the way, we spoke of our upcoming final examinations and our plans for higher education. Only when we got tired and sat down on a bench to rest did Viktor tell me that he had liked me for a long time, that he had grown fond of me, and asked if he may kiss me. Well, how could I not permit it when my heart yearned for him! He kissed me so carefully and tenderly on the cheek, and then put his arm around my shoulders. We sat silently for a long time, each of us inwardly experiencing our first happiness together, our love.

After that, we saw each other every day as we prepared for our final examinations. We passed them easily. Viktor received the highest grades and was awarded the special letter of commendation. In addition, at the prom following graduation, the director of the school handed Viktor a letter of gratitude and congratulations signed by himself and all the teachers. Soon after that final evening, Father took us all away to L'viv, and I parted from Viktor for five long years.

Maria Rudenko-Kramchaninova

6

Military Mountaineering, Moscow Air School, War's Beginning

Viktor Kramchaninov

The joyful visions lasted not;
Her musings now depict
A country by the Lord forgot:
A master harsh and strict.

From *Princess Troubetzkoy* by N. A. Nekrasov (1821-1878)[15]

א

When I was still seventeen, I and other graduates were called to the army enlistment office at Zhitomyr city hall. We had been prepared by our oft-repeated slogan: "I am ready for work and defense!" All over Ukraine, military-related sports became popular. Young men and women in high school participated in running, jumping, swimming, shooting, and throwing inactive hand grenades. Students were trained to drive vehicles, ride motorcycles, and even to become pilots and parachutists. I had training in combat and had learned to handle and shoot a rifle. Societies for assisting the army, navy and air force sprang up like mushrooms. Youthful confidence surged. "The Soviet people are afraid of no one! Let someone try to attack us; we will repulse them! Stalin will not allow war, but if it begins, we will quickly and easily triumph! We will

15 Published in English translation by Soskice (1977, p 9).

fight—for Stalin—for the Motherland." As a result of my training and enthusiasm, I was assigned to train other, older recruits.

Apparently, I was a good instructor, for soon I received the prized assignment to learn military mountaineering at Camp Science in the Caucasus Mountains, which lie between the Black and the Caspian Seas. Initially, I went to Kiev where I joined a group of students from the Railway Institute. Then, we traveled by train through Donetsk and Rostov. After crossing back and forth over the cold, muddy Kuban River to Nevinnomyssk, we left the train and continued by bus to Cherkessk. From there we walked south for about forty miles through the towns of Karachaevsk and Tiberda and up the Dombai valley. Now, for the first time, I saw the magnificent and high Caucasus Mountains; they made an indelible impression upon me.

We pitched our tents in the shadow of Mount Dombai-Ulgen, which is more than 13,000 feet high and is on the border with Georgia. The Dombai-Ulgen River, a torrent flowing directly from the Aliback glacier, provided us with frigid bath water. We ate canned food and chocolate and drank coffee. Each day we arose promptly at six and followed a strict schedule. On the first day, we received our climbing equipment—ice ax, ropes, backpack, boots with crampons, down sleeping bags, pitons, rifles, dark glasses, and tents—with a total weight of sixty-six pounds. With the packs on our backs, we began training by walking the mountain trails. Then came progressively more difficult terrain, trudging up grassy slopes, climbing moraines, and scrambling up scree, the loose rock lying on steep inclines.

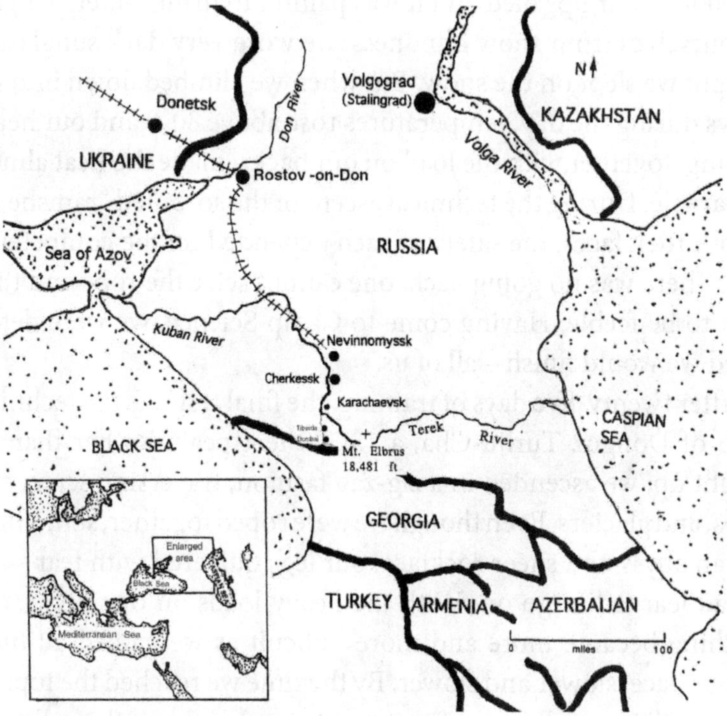

Geographical sketch of the Caucasus region. Shown is the railway (crosshatched line) from Donetsk to Nevinnomyssk. The Kuban River rises near Mt. Elbrus, Europe's tallest mountain (18,513 feet). Viktor's group camped near the village of Dombai, in the Karachai-Cherkessk district, on the border with Georgia, west of Mt. Elbrus. Karachai are peoples of Turkish descent, and the Cherkessk are Caucasian in origin. Also shown are Stalingrad, the Terek River and the city of Baku.

Finally, when our instructor felt we had enough experience, had improved our physical endurance, and could cope with fear, we were roped together for technical climbing across deep rock clefts and up vertical cliffs. There was the glacier where crevasses thirty meters deep might be hidden beneath snow bridges too fragile to bear human weight. And there were other charms: because of the dry air and the intensity of the ultraviolet light at altitudes above

10,000 feet, our lips bled and it was painful to drink water. To protect ourselves from snow blindness, we wore very dark sunglasses. At night we slept on the snow. But when we climbed down into the valleys during the day, temperatures rose above 80 °F and our heavy clothing, together with the load on our backs, made the heat almost unbearable. During the technical ascent of the so-called "ramshead" smooth rock faces, the safety of each depended on the competence of all. There was no going back; one cannot seize the rope and then claim to be feeble. Having come to Camp Science, we were determined we would finish—all of us.

After twenty-five days of training, the final test was the technical climb of Donguz-Turlju-Cha, a 13,500 feet peak. Rather than go straight up, we ascended in a zig-zag fashion, traversing scree, crevasses, and glaciers. Even though we were roped together, sometimes over an abyss or a sheer rockface, our legs quivered with fear—but we had learned to go on. With the heavy loads on our backs, our breathing became more and more difficult as we gained altitude, and our pace, slower and slower. By the time we reached the top, we were crawling on all fours. But when I stood and saw the valley far below, the mountains rising on each side, the snow-covered peaks sparkling in the sun, and the clouds floating beneath me, I forgot my fatigue. I saw the birds, just visible, circling in the distance far below us. For many minutes I stood, entranced. Surrounded by this beauty, the weeks of training and the perils of our climb suddenly became worthwhile. Our instructor, a Karachai by birth, proudly announced in his native tongue the names of the visible peaks: "Ine," "Kazbek," and "Kara-Kaya." From within a pyramid made of stones, we removed the canister holding the list of the previous summiteers, and added our names to document our success.

Graduates of Camp Science. Viktor is second from the right in the first row of four. The local climbing instructor is wearing the traditional Karachai hat and holding an ice ax in his right hand. Young women, being trained in military mountaineering, attended Camp Science. In Soviet times, women were also expected to handle weapons, fly planes, drive motorcycles, and, as here, climb mountains.

After an exhilarating mountaintop experience, the descent was dreary. As a result of muscle fatigue, our legs gave way, but, clinging to rocks with our arms, we descended without falling. Fortunately, we were allowed to rest the following day. That night, we stood solemnly in line for the award ceremony, as each was presented with the prized badge of "USSR Mountaineer, First Class," emblazoned with an image of the "Kazbek" mountain and a golden ice ax. Then, warmed both by the large campfire and the comradeship of these difficult days, we recounted our experiences, sang songs, and recited our favorite pieces. I recited some lines that had come to me when I stood at the summit and looked eastward toward the origin of the Terek River as it begins its race to the Caspian Sea. The lines were from Pushkin's poem *Onegin's Journey*, and they spoke of the grandeur of the Caucasus Mountains, the endurance of the Terek River, and the recurrence of war.

He sees proud Terek, magisterial,
gnaw the steep confines of its bed;
up here an eagle planes, imperial,
a stag stands there with lowered head....

Far off loom the Caucasian masses;
their road is open. War has pried
its way through their age-old divide
across their barriers and crevasses.[16]

I had no idea then how nearly prophetic Pushkin's lines were, for in September 1942, just two years after I left Camp Science, the German drive into the Caucasus to gain access to the rich oilfields would be finally blocked by the Soviet Army at the Terek River.

After returning to Zhitomyr, I worked briefly with Father as a motor vehicle mechanic, while I waited for the outcome of my application for pilot training. In a few days, I was ordered to report to the Moscow Air School, where I would become a cadet, not in pilot training, but in telecommunications. When I arrived at the Air School, I found the military discipline even more strict than at Camp Science. I was as a galloping stallion being suddenly reined in to a halt. Those cadets who were not accustomed to hard work, something which had been my diet since early childhood, were soon ordered to regular army units. Now I appreciated my parents' strict discipline. When, as a fully-fledged cadet, I was given our very smart regimental uniforms, I sent a photo to Maria, for we corresponded regularly.

16 Published in English translation by Charles Johnson (1983, p4).

Photograph of Viktor, inscribed on the back, "To my darling Maria from a cadet of the First Moscow Holding the Order of the Red Banner Military Flying School. June 25, 1940."

For basic training in combat, we were taken about sixty miles south of Moscow to a summer military camp on the Oka River. The camp was near a Cossack village, Belopesotskaya, named for its white sand. Each day, in full uniform, we were taught combat tactics and ran for six miles along the river. For equipment we each carried a bag holding three hand grenades weighing one and a half pounds each, a rifle, and a gas mask. There were also ammunition belts, a bag with three cartridge clips, a sleeping bag, greatcoat, shovel, and canteen. Maneuvers required that we crawl on the sand carrying this pack. Our shirts became wet with sweat but stiff with salt on drying. Every day, we bathed and washed our clothes in the river. Fortunately, we had plenty of good food. Rice pilaf was my favorite. Day by day we grew stronger and more robust.

By October 1940, when we began our class work, we were in superb physical condition. The rigid schedule continued, but now with the addition of study. Ours was the premier military academy in the entire Moscow district. When important foreign military visitors came to the Soviet Union, they visited us. General Charles de Gaulle of France visited, and I remember how he peered intently into our faces as he passed along the line. He knew the challenges we would face, more than we did ourselves, and he wanted to see if we were up to the task. On those Sundays when we were given leave, I visited the museums, galleries, and exhibitions in Moscow, and attended the famous Bolshoi Opera and Ballet Theater and the Maliy Theater. In the evenings at the camp I sang in the chorus, where we learned a lot of Russian national songs.

In 1941, as May First approached, we began preparations for the great parade in Moscow's Red Square. We practiced each night at the main airfield, accompanied by a band. Our column, which followed that of the Air Academy, consisted of four hundred cadets—twenty rows of twenty men each. I was in charge of the first row, and all of the cadets followed my cue. We did a very precise goose step, carrying our rifles on our left shoulders, and having a sharp wave of the right arm. On May Day, our battalion passed Lenin's tomb, moving in unison as though we were one man. For the first time I saw, high above, Stalin, Molotov, Budjoniy, Voroshilov, and other leaders. My pride in our country was indescribable. Whatever the challenge, we would meet it!

The day after the parade, the Moscow Military District Commander-in-Chief issued an official congratulation to our school, and the day after that we were transferred back to the summer camp on the Oka River. There we resumed very intense training in aircraft engine maintenance, operation of radio stations, gunnery, and navigation. The scent of war was in the air: the assignments were made tougher, the training was accelerated, and the length of the working day was increased to twelve hours.

On 22 June 1941, I stood night watch near the armory, peering vigilantly into the impenetrable pitch. In the morning, while catching up on my sleep, the loudspeaker awakened me with its stark, terse message:

"The war has begun!"

As one of four cadets who had already passed the examinations, I immediately submitted an official request to the army for assignment to the front. I was given the rank of sergeant and put in charge of fourteen soldiers. We were assigned to the radio station of the Forty-fifth Air Army, at Krotovo near Moscow, and charged with communication for the Soviet fleet of long-range bombers. Our responsibility was to maintain communication with the four-engine heavy bombers, the TB-7 and the subsequent model, the Pe-8, which flew night missions far beyond the front lines to Kaliningrad and even Berlin. These aircraft carried either ten or eleven crew and up to six tons of bombs, and conducted bombing raids on enemy troop concentrations, weapons depots, equipment warehouses, fuel storage sites, railroad junctions, airports, and Baltic Sea shipping. When our ground troops were in difficulty, the bombers went into action along the battle line. When the planes were returning from a mission, we used radio beams to guide them back to our airfield through the darkness and fog.

Soon, nine female wireless operators were assigned to my group. As their commanding officer, I heard from these women many heart-breaking stories. They were in the military, but I had never before had women under my command. I was not quite sure how to proceed, but decided on equal discipline for men and women. For example, if a woman said that she was not fit for duty, but could not give an acceptable reason, then her request was refused and she went to her post. One night, while doing a security check at our radio station, I saw a sentry kissing one of our radio operators, his rifle propped up against a tree some distance away. I gave both a severe reprimand, sent the soldier back to his post, and the woman back to her quarters. It was sufficient discipline. The women performed disheartening, demanding work, and they were dedicated to their tasks. While on duty, they remained at their stations until all the planes had returned or were accounted for, and they made sure to maintain radio communication with the aircraft throughout.

For the remainder of 1941, with our country on the defensive in the darkest days of the war, our group of heavy bomber squadrons functioned continuously. During this time, I received two ominous letters from my brother, Nikolai, who was on leave from the Economic Institute in Odessa and was spending the summer with Natalia and her family in Gorlovka. There was no word from our parents and the German Army was rapidly advancing in Ukraine.

Gorlovka
21 August 1941

Be well, Viktor!

Thanks for your letters of August 7 and 12 and the one postcard, but I've not yet received any notification of the money you sent. There is no word from our parents; maybe we can have them moved farther east. On August 17, I wrote to Moscow Migration Management.[17] *You write too, because you are closer to Moscow. I wrote to my Institute in Odessa, but got no answer; I think it is impossible for me to return there to study.*[18] *Maybe I will go to the Economics Institute in Saratov.*[19] *So far life hasn't changed, but if the enemy comes we will all volunteer and the Donbass will become a grave for German fascism. I*

17 Viktor's parents could not move, because German troops had already occupied Zhitomyr on 9 July 1941.

18 Odessa was already threatened by the German Army.

19 Saratov is a city on the Volga River about two hundred miles north of Stalingrad and was not occupied by German forces during the war.

continue to work loading railway freight cars; two loaded with metal were sent out yesterday.[20]

Egor [Bulgakov, Natalia's husband] *was moved to the machinery plant. Yuri and Julia* [Natalia's children] *are already big. Julia* [born 1940] *is not walking yet, but Yuri* [born 1939] *has already learned foul language. Today Katerina brought us honey. They live well, but she is not yet working. Uncle Arhip wrote that he was in battles near Belaya Tserkov* [sixty miles south of Kiev]. *Otherwise things are well.*

Regards,
Nikolai

P.S. Egor was recruited today and I have received papers for tomorrow. Write more often, please!

Gorlovka
29 September 1941

Be well, Viktor!

We got your postcard, thanks. I continue to work at the same place, but as there are no railway cars anymore, I have less to do. Last month I earned 485 rubles, and this month it will be no more than 350, so there will be little money for vodka. We have received the cards rationing bread and tomorrow will get those for groceries. We have salted away some cucumbers and tomatoes, and will get some potatoes and cabbage if we get paid in advance. Today it is snowing,

20 To preserve its productive capacity for the war effort, the Soviet Union dismantled whole Ukrainian industries, transported them to safety east of the Ural Mountains and reassembled them. Nikolai and Egor were involved in the dismantling process in the Donbass.

but I have no winter shoes or clothes as my things are still at the Institute in Odessa.

Tomorrow, Uncle Ivan's wife, Lena, will join the Labor Army, and the day after I go for Universal Military Training. I will get better training there than in the Home Guard, though that was not wasted. The enemy is now inside the Donbass. The "front" is just around the corner. Still no word from our parents.

With regards,
Nikolai

Then, in the first part of 1942, I myself was called upon for a most unusual mission.

Viktor P. Kramchaninov

7

I Monitored Molotov's Wartime Flight

Viktor Kramchaninov

... when there's some new triumph in war
victorious Russia's celebrating ...

From *The Bronze Horseman* by Alexander S. Pushkin (1799-1837)[21]

א

During these desperate times, I was personally involved in an event often overlooked in the history of the Great Patriotic War—Foreign Minister Molotov's flight to Great Britain and the United States of America. For ten years after its successful completion, it was kept under the strictest secrecy in the Soviet Union. Even in subsequent years, many details have not been disclosed. As is known, after America entered the war in December 1941, the US and Britain were allies of the Soviet Union in the struggle against fascism, and Soviet diplomats in London had worked hard to create a coalition. In the early months of 1942, the Soviet army was under great pressure, with the enemy at the gates of Moscow, Leningrad under siege, Ukraine occupied, and Stalingrad in the south being threatened by a rapid German advance. The military situation was grim.

21 Published in English translation by Charles Johnson (1983, p40).

On 12 April 1942, Stalin received a message from President Franklin Roosevelt of the United States, asking Vyacheslav Molotov, Minister of Foreign Affairs, accompanied by appropriate military representatives, to come to Washington to discuss joint tactics. On 20 April, Stalin agreed. Two TB-7 long-range bombers from our Forty-fifth Air Army were removed from combat duties. By order of Stalin, one plane commanded by Major Sergey Asyamov was selected for the mission. The co-pilot was Major Endell Puusepp.

Because of their prior polar explorations, both Asyamov and Puusepp were well-known, experienced Arctic pilots. In addition to Molotov, they would carry the Vice-President of the National Committee for Defense of the Soviet Union. Including the pilots, there were thirteen crewmembers: navigators (Shtepenko and Romanov), flight engineers (Dmitriev and Zolotarjov), bombardier-gunner (Goncharov), gunners (Kozhin, Salnikov, Smirnov, and Belousov), and radio operators (Nizovtsev and Muhanov).

At 7:00 PM on 28 April 1942, by personal order of Stalin, the plane left the Ramenskoe Airbase bound for Scotland. During the entire flight, I maintained radio contact with Muhanov. Communication remained very clear, both for me and for Marshal Golovanov in Moscow who, as Stalin's personal representative, was also monitoring the flight. Using oxygen masks at altitudes up to 26,000 feet, the plane flew over Germany, once experiencing anti-aircraft fire as it crossed the battlefront. Nine hours after take-off, it landed safely at Tealing Airfield, in Angus County, near Dundee in Scotland.

From Tealing, a special train took Molotov to London. The bomber remained at Tealing, and Asyamov was transferred as a passenger to a de Havilland Flamingo airplane, which took off for London. During the flight from Scotland to London, the plane carrying Asyamov exploded in mid-air and all on board, including the Soviet military attaché to Britain, Colonel Pugachjov, were lost.[22] In London, the meetings with Churchill, Molotov, and the Soviet Ambassador to Britain, Maisky, concluded with an agreement to sign a future Mutual Assistance Pact, whereby Britain and the Soviet Union would cooperate in the war, and Britain and the Western powers would open a second front in Europe. Following these meetings, and with Stalin having designated that Puusepp should replace Asyamov as captain for the flight, the TB-7 departed from Tealing for the United States. The navigators chose a route to Washington via Reykjavik, Iceland, and Gander, Newfoundland. From Scotland, they flew at 10,000 feet through turbulent storms. Although the runway in Reykjavik was quite short, they were able to land safely.

From Reykjavik the route across the North Atlantic to Newfoundland was more than 1,700 miles, the longest leg of their journey. The morning following their arrival in Reykjavik, after the flight engineer, Dmitriev, had completely filled all fuel tanks, it was necessary to offload one ton of fuel. Otherwise, with the short runway, the plane would have been too heavy to lift off. Even so, Puusepp later told me how narrowly they escaped disaster getting the heavily-laden plane airborne. On the left of the runway was a high snow bank, and on the right, a line of Catalina type aircraft. The runway ended over the ocean, and there was a strong side-wind. With the plane under full throttle, as it began to lift, the wind blew it to the right toward the parked planes. To avoid collision, Puusepp turned the plane slightly to the left, but then the undercarriage brushed the snow bank, causing him to lose altitude. He was almost

22 Given the secrecy and suspicion that surrounded the air crash, Viktor would not know all the details. The DH.95 Flamingo R2764 carrying the pilot Azyamov and three other Soviet officials crashed on 30 April, near Great Ouseburn, Yorkshire. On 1 May Major Pussep flew the Soviet bomber back to Moscow. Probably suspecting sabotage, Stalin cabled Roosevelt on 14 May that Molotov's flight would be delayed because of "weather". Stalin must have satisfied himself that the crash was accidental, for on 20 May Churchill cabled Roosevelt, "Molotov arrived" (Ruffle 2001, Sherwood 1950, Young 2001).

down to the water when the plane slowly began to gain altitude. "Glory be to God!" Puusepp whispered. "We made it!"

As they were now flying through the clouds in very cold temperatures, the plane began to ice up, and it was necessary to decrease altitude. When the plane was over Greenland, the message came in from Newfoundland that the airport at Gander was closed due to fog, and that they had to land three hundred miles to the northwest at a newly opened airport in Goose Bay. The route change was promptly made by the navigators Romanov and Shtepenko. For the last leg of the journey the flight controllers in Washington, D.C. prescribed the low altitude of 3,300 feet. It was very warm on the eastern seaboard that day, and all the engines began to overheat. To prevent fire, Dmitriev, the flight engineer, had to switch off engine number three on the right wing. When the other three engines continued to overheat, he requested that Puusepp decrease the airspeed. Fortunately, the temperatures of the remaining working engines stabilized. Flying slowly on three engines, the plane limped into Washington and landed safely, to the great relief of Molotov, who praised the crew for their fine work.

There followed a reception at the White House. Puusepp and crew were also invited, and their photograph together with President Roosevelt and Foreign Minister Molotov became a proudly treasured souvenir. During the conferences, Molotov and Roosevelt agreed on an interest-free loan from the United States to the Soviet Union of one billion dollars, and on military cooperation in Europe, including the opening of a second front.

A photograph circa 1966 of Viktor, second from left, with the famed Captain, now Colonel, Puusep, fourth from left in beard and glasses. Puusepp successfully completed the flight bearing Molotov to the west during 1942. Later in the war, while flying a Pe-8 Soviet four-engine bomber, Puusepp and navigator Shtepenko were credited with extraordinarily accurate bombing of enemy installations. After the war, Puusepp, an Estonian, became president of the Estonian Aero Club (Ruffle, 2001).

After leaving Washington, clouds, ice, snow, and rainsqualls forced the plane to maintain a rather low altitude to Goose Bay and on to Iceland. For their return journey from Britain to the Soviet Union, the British suggested the crew take a southern route, by way of Egypt, but the offer was refused since the route over Europe was probably open[23], and because the engines might overheat again in warm weather.

23 Pussep commented on their strategy for a safe return in his January 1986 article published in the magazine *Wings of the Motherland*. [For an excerpt from this article, see Appendix B.]

When Puusepp flew over German-occupied territory, his plane would have been within the range of enemy fighters, so this last leg of the journey was the most dangerous, but fortunately the enemy missed their chance. In early June, Molotov was safely back in Moscow. In official announcements, the Soviet news agency, *TASS*, reported that Molotov had been in Britain and the United States and that our allies would open a second front in the West. For completing the flight successfully, Captain Puusepp and the two navigators, Shtepenko and Romanov, were given our country's highest military honor, "Hero of the Soviet Union," and the other crewmembers received the "Battle Order of the Red Banner."

Some years later, Puusepp told me some startling details. One was Stalin's personal and private order to him as the pilot: If the aircraft was about to go down in German-occupied territory, Puusepp was to shoot Molotov and throw his body out of the plane, through the bomb bay doors. Apparently, there were secrets attached to this mission that even Molotov did not know.

Viktor Kramchaninov

8

The Battle of Kursk—1943

Viktor Kramchaninov

The roads that lead to my Ukraine
Are overgrown with thorns profane
It may be I have left her shore
Forever and forever more!

From *To A.Y. Kozachkovsky* by Taras Shevchenko (1814-1861)[24]

א

I hated the Nazis so much for the crisis they had brought upon my loved ones and our country that in the summer of 1942 I volunteered for combat, even though I knew the risks. I had seen our planes return, bringing the wounded and bodies of the dead with them. I had heard over our radio the final words of my friends in doomed bombers. I suffered each time one of our planes did not return to base. I would take my chances; dread of the wolf would not keep me from going into the dark forest. 1941 and 1942 were our darkest years. My Maria, her family and mine, were somewhere in occupied Ukraine. Were they alive and safe? I wanted to fight for them, for the Motherland, for Stalin! I requested an official transfer to a combat bomber.

24 Published in English translation by Andrusyshen and Kirkconnell, (1963, p 99). Taras Shevchenko was one of Viktor's favorite, and one of Ukraine's greatest, poets.

Viktor Kramchaninov, 1943, as a radio operator and navigator, wearing his flight helmet and his fur-lined flight jacket.

My request for transfer was accepted, and I was assigned as the radio operator-navigator to Captain Vihorev's four-engine heavy bomber and began flying combat missions. We flew four missions to the Pulkovo Heights where, at the village of Bezzabotniy, close to Peterhof, the German Army had set up artillery batteries which fired into the besieged city of Leningrad. In spite of heavy anti-aircraft fire, we dropped demolition bombs on their artillery emplacements. We also flew missions to Voronezh, nearly five hundred miles south of Moscow, and to the steppe. Our missions over Stalingrad helped bring victory in that battle.[25] In the spring of 1943, we faced the next German offensive.

25 Marshal Zhukov, the Soviet Commander, considered the recapture on September 16 of the strategic hill, Mamayev Kurgan, to be the turning point of the Stalingrad battle, the turning point of the war. His memoirs credit Viktor's squadron for key air strikes. Viktor may have contributed to the precise turning point of World War II.

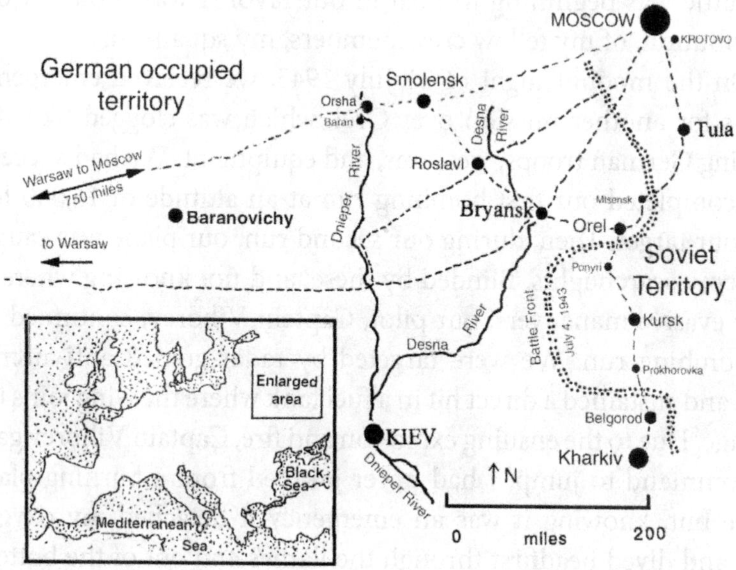

Geographical sketch of the Kursk battlefront (shown as double dotted lines) before the German attack on 5 July, 1943. Their attack from Orel was stopped at Ponri, and the attack from Belgorod was stopped at Prokhorovka. Some of the major highways are shown as dashed lines, but accompanying rail lines are not shown.

Our victory at Stalingrad in February had left the city of Kursk in the center of a great westward bulge in the battle lines. Hitler thought a pincer movement from Orel in the north and Belgorod in the south would trap the Soviet Army and open the way to Moscow. In a huge gamble, he organized nearly all his available forces for an attack on Kursk. In preparation, the enemy assembled men and matériel in Orel, which we bombed, and our crew was decorated for its action. The attack began on the fifth of July 1943, but the Soviet army under Marshal Zhukov had prepared strong defenses. Once the battle began, we flew missions to destroy the enemy's equipment and damage its supply lines. By mid-July, we could see that the battle was beginning to turn in our favor. I was proud of our contribution, of my fellow crewmembers, my squadron.

On the moonlit night of 21 July 1943, we received emergency orders for another mission over Orel, which was clogged by withdrawing German troops, weapons, and equipment. We had successfully completed our first bombing run at an altitude of 16,000 feet over our target. Then, during our second run, our plane was caught in enemy searchlights. Blinded by these, and not knowing where to make evasive maneuvers, our pilot, Captain Vihorev, continued on the bombing run. We were targeted by radar-guided anti-aircraft guns, and sustained a direct hit in a fuel tank where the wing joins the fuselage. Due to the ensuing explosion and fire, Captain Vihorev gave the command to jump. I had never jumped from a burning plane before but, knowing it was an emergency, I detached my oxygen hose, and dived headfirst through the flames and out of the bottom hatch. On the way out, my head hit something, but fortunately, being protected by my flight helmet, I did not lose consciousness.

The crew of Viktor's four-engine heavy bomber. He is third from the right. In front is Nick, a war orphan, who had been adopted by the crew. Soviet airmen frequently adopted such orphans during the war.

Because we were at such high altitude, I decided to free-fall for as long as possible to diminish the amount of time I would be in the air. Falling at more than a hundred miles per hour, I could not pressurize my ears, and I cried out with pain. Spiraling downward, I could see the ground and the flashes of the anti-aircraft guns. When I groped for the ring to release my parachute, it was not there! As the ground rapidly approached, fear gripped me and my hair stood on end, as though to lift my helmet. I grabbed my flying suit where the ring should be and pulled with all my might—so hard that I tore off a piece of the leather, which came right out in my hand! Silk glided by my ear. My parachute opened!

Suddenly, all was silence around me. My parachute had opened and I was hanging in the air, floating gently toward the earth. I was alive and unhurt, and now could take stock of my situation. As I hung onto the straps of my parachute and looked around, I saw our plane crash to the ground in flames. I was surrounded by the battle of Kursk and behind German lines with no chance of landing in Soviet-controlled territory. I saw that I was drifting toward the city of Orel, which our planes were continuing to bomb. If I landed there, Nazi soldiers could capture me, and I would immediately be shot. By manipulating pull on the straps, I changed the direction of my descent away from Orel and toward a dark area below, but now the ground was rushing toward me at great speed. Before striking the earth, I released the straps to slow my descent and just had time to cross my hands and legs and curl myself into a ball. The impact almost knocked the wind out of me. I got out of my harness and jumped up as fast as possible. To my surprise, I was okay! My arms, hands, feet and legs were unharmed.

Up until now, I had never confronted an enemy soldier. It was two o'clock in the morning, and I had landed in ripening rye growing in a field half a mile wide. In the bright moonlight, the white parachute was easily visible as it floated on the waving grain. Roads ran along each side of the field. When Nazi soldiers who were driving by saw the parachute, they stopped their vehicle and five of them jumped out and ran toward it. I crawled away as fast as I could, keeping low on all fours. But as I approached the road on the opposite side of the field, a motorcycle carrying two Nazi soldiers roared to a stop and they ran toward where I was hidden, crouched low in the rye. Now, for the first time, I was face to face with the enemy.

Hastily, I loaded my pistol and, as we had been trained in maneuvers, waited until the two soldiers were quite near. I fired two quick shots at them. They fell. I jumped over them and ran. Now I was completely exposed. I ran faster than ever before in my life. If there was ever a time when the months of physical training paid off, it was then. With my heart pounding in my throat, I ran through fields, forests, and ravines for about four miles. When I finally sank down exhausted and looked around, I saw a figure in a flying suit, pistol in hand, approaching me. I stood up, clasping my own pistol. After a moment's hesitation, we recognized each other. He was Arkadiy Zabolotsky, the flight engineer on our plane. After a brief greeting and a quick conference, we decided we must go east to find our side, and try to cross the front. It was too dangerous to stay in enemy territory, with the German army all around us. As the Orel-Kursk battle had already been raging for sixteen days, the front was no longer continuous, so we might be able to find a gap where there was little shooting and where we could sneak through.

We had not gone far when the day began to dawn. Knowing we could not chance walking by daylight, and seeing some bushes ahead, we hid in them as best we could. When we sought this cover, we had paid no attention to several huge mounds that lay just beyond our thicket but, with the dawn, we saw piles of German corpses that no one had buried. About three hundred yards beyond these was a dirt road, on which columns of enemy tanks, trucks, and soldiers were moving toward the front. As the sun rose, the heat became intolerable, the corpses stank, and we were tormented by thirst. Dark blue flies landed on our faces to drink our sweat and black flies stabbed our skin to drink our blood, but to move a muscle to wave them off would risk giving ourselves away. All day long till evening we lay on our backs in the sun, the whole time wearing our flight helmets and our fur flying suits. In the months to come, I would be in many battles and would come closer to death, but for me this day, 22 July 1943, was the vilest day of the war. Never before had I hated fascists or war so deeply. Even now, decades later, I can recall no other day of the war for which I harbor such revulsion.

Finally, that night, when all was dark, we gladly left the thicket and, finding a stretch of the front without gunfire, we successfully crossed over to our own troops. We were greeted by a sergeant in the infantry who said he had seen our plane go down in flames. After both Zabolotsky and I had drunk two canteens of water, the sergeant gave us each two bowls of soup made from concentrate. Nothing had ever tasted so good.

Aircrews were vital to our war effort and there was a standing order not to detain airmen. A lieutenant showed us on the map how to reach Tula nearly a hundred miles to the north. He gave us each a loaf of bread, a container of dried herring, and a canteen of water. After thanking him for his kindness and saying good-byes, we began to walk. The German Army was now retreating, and we walked through remains of villages that our army had re-captured. Much of Mtsensk lay in ruins. For miles of countryside, there were shell holes and tank tracks everywhere, with hardly a trace of vegetation. All habitation was destroyed; only here and there a chimney marked where a house once stood. Although we later learned the staggering magnitude of the German defeat, we could see with our own eyes that a huge battle had taken place. It was not hard to believe that second only to Stalingrad, Kursk was the largest battle in all of World War II.

Sometimes we hitched a ride with a truck carrying wounded soldiers, but mostly we walked, leaving Mtsensk and the worst of the battle-scarred earth behind us. We entered more pleasant countryside. Forests appeared. Occasionally there were green fields under cultivation, and even some gardens with fruit trees where we refreshed ourselves with green apples. After several days, walking northeastward through the towns of Chern and Plavsk, we arrived at Tula. This ancient Russian city had already achieved fame in the war. Residents told us how they had worked side-by-side with the Soviet Army in November 1941 and blocked the German advance on Moscow from the south. Their city had protected Moscow again, they said, just as it had had stopped the Tartars in 1552.

From the airport at Tula we were flown to our own airbase, located thirteen miles southeast of Moscow in Krotovo. When we arrived, imagine the tumultuous reunion with our friends! Being tired and hungry, how we relished a good meal! And vodka. Airmen were well-housed and fed, and vodka, an important symbol for our army, was in abundance. If a crew successfully completed ten missions, each man was awarded five hundred rubles, enough to buy a bottle of vodka. Before a ground assault, our infantry received an extra ration. For the airmen, when the crew came into the dining room after returning from a mission, on the table at each place was a six-ounce glass of vodka and, beside it, a piece of bread. If a man was considered lost, the glass was covered with the bread and remained there until his loss was confirmed. Zabolotsky and I had the great satisfaction of drinking our vodka with our fellow crewmembers in celebration of our return. Miraculously, even though our plane had been shot down behind enemy lines, eight of our original crew had returned safely and unharmed. One of these was our pilot, Captain Alexey Vihorev, who held the country's highest military honor—"Hero of the Soviet Union." Only three of our crew had been lost. So far in the battle of the Orel-Kursk bulge, our squadron had lost ten bombers, including ours, to anti-aircraft fire.

While preparations were being made to obtain a new bomber, we had a few days of recuperation at our airbase. During this time, there was an amusing incident involving our regimental political deputy. Early in the war I had joined the Communist Party and, at that time, membership was a great honor and a great responsibility. As only the best people could be admitted, I was very proud. Yet to tell the truth, I did not like many of the Party officials. One was our political deputy. In all regiments in the Soviet Army, there was a special deputy commander for politics who was usually, as in our case, an aggressive and ambitious, but lazy and ignorant, small-time politician. Our regiment got as much good from our deputy as milk from a billy goat! The deputy knew nothing of aviation, but lounged about everywhere, eavesdropping for tidbits he could report to the higher Party officials. One day I was sitting with my friends, watching the airplanes take-off and land. Then, I noticed this political deputy lurking behind a tree listening to our conversation. I gave a wink to my buddies, and then very seriously pointed to a plane which had just left the ground, its wheels still spinning prior to being retracted into the fuselage. "Look," I said loudly, "that lousy Ivanov has just left the ground, but he forgot to switch off the wheels." At the Party meeting the next day, the deputy took the floor. "At this time of crisis, when our entire country is fighting for its life, pilot Ivanov is squandering valuable fuel by failing to switch off the wheels after takeoff." Laughter erupted and lasted for many minutes. A few days later, the political deputy was recalled from the regiment. This made an entertaining story that I often told, and would later think about, but at the time I thought no more of it—we had a war to fight.

Soon, our crew received three new members and we were flown five hundred miles due east of Moscow to the airplane factory at Kazan, where we waited for several more days to obtain our new Pe-8 model bomber. While waiting, we had the great pleasure of participating in the marriage of Captain Vihorev to his fiancée, Zoya. She had come from her village near Moscow to join him in Kazan. After getting the bomber, we put Zoya aboard as though she were a member of the crew, and we flew back to our base. Zoya returned to her home village and we, to combat duty—night bombing runs.

On the night of 27 August 1943, we received emergency orders to bomb a build-up of fascist troops and armor at the rail junction of Roslavl. As we approached our target, the sound of our engines caused the enemy to activate their anti-aircraft batteries and searchlights, and there were a great many of both. Anti-aircraft shells were exploding at altitudes between 13,000 and 16,500 feet, where our planes, with their five tons of bombs, were operating. Maneuvering between the flack bursts, we made our first bombing run on the railroad junction. On our second run, we dropped our bombs precisely. We hit the enemy, not on the eyebrow, but in the eye, directly on the rail terminal itself, igniting several fires. Our battle plan called for yet another pass over the target, this time dropping thermite flares, which burn brightly at 5,000°F. As they descended slowly by parachute, the flares would illuminate the target for the next wave of our bombers.

But as we made our third run over the target, we sustained a direct hit, setting us on fire. The explosion had jammed the escape hatch on the bottom of the fuselage. It was impossible to jump. There was no escape! As the plane dived, it went into a roll which pushed my back against the oxygen cylinders with such force that I could not move. We were falling from 16,000 feet and I waited for certain death, which I knew would come within four minutes. It's true: under such circumstances, your whole life passes before your eyes. Then, I passed out.

Viktor P. Kramchaninov

9

Partisans, an American B-25, and War's End

Viktor Kramchaninov

There yet will come a time when Truth will speak
And smash our evil edifice of woes;
Till then, sound loudly, Kobza, in our land,
And nearer bring God's Doomsday on our foes!

From *Prelude* by Panteleimon Kulish (1819-1897)[26]

א

As we spiraled downward, the stresses on the damaged bomber caused it to break apart in midair, and I fell out. When the hard jet of cold air hit my face I came to, just in time to pull the ring of my parachute. I don't recall striking the ground, but awoke lying in a forest, with my parachute strung up on a tree and our bomber burning nearby. When I tried to get up, intense pain caused me to pass out again.

When I came to, it was daybreak. To my relief, I could move my arms and legs, but I had broken some ribs, my hands and face were burned, and my right arm was badly lacerated. My situation seemed hopeless—I was lying wounded in a forest behind enemy lines, far

26 Published in English translation by Andrusyshen and Kirkconnell (1963, p158). The *kobza*, a predecessor of the modern bandura, is a lute-like instrument used by ancient Ukrainian bards to accompany poetic recitations.

from the front. If found, I would be shot. We say, "Seven disasters, but only one response." I had to get away from this spot. My hatred for the Nazis, who had brought such great harm to my country, made me realize that I must live to fight this enemy again—for Maria, my family, the Motherland—and for Stalin.

I knew that in these forests near Roslavl and Bryansk, there were partisans.[27] This region was poor and sparsely populated, but the people were such devoted Communists that it was called the "red belt" of Russia. I must reach the partisans, no matter what the effort. To get more energy, I ate the bar of chocolate from the pocket of my flying jacket. After an hour I could make small movements of my arms, legs and head, even though each movement brought pain. I forced myself to my feet. There was a stick nearby and, leaning on it, I managed to walk and found a path leading through the trees.

The early morning sun bore down and my throat was parched for lack of water. I slowly made my way through the heat of the day and, by the afternoon, I came upon a thatched cottage in a clearing. Luck was with me. Partisans lived here. In this remarkable household there were the father, Phillip Kuznetsov, his wife Anna, their adult sons, Anton and Basil, their teenage sons, Viktor and Peter, their daughters Efrosinja and Anjuta, and their daughter-in-law, Maria Maljutina.[28] The two older brothers worked on the railroad, but were members of the partisans. The family hated the enemy and had great faith in our ultimate victory. How well I remember them. Even now, as I write their names, tears of excitement, love, and gratitude dim my eyes. They knew well that the Nazis shot anyone sheltering our airmen, and yet they received me. As I entered their

---

27 Partisan bands were formed by patriotic residents in Nazi occupied territory and thousands of Soviet soldiers, who had evaded capture, or were dropped by air behind the front lines. These bands effectively harrassed enemy rail and road transport, such that in winter the Germans were forced to the costly expedient of supplying their troops by air.

28 On the 26th of July 1966, Peter Kuznetsov and his sister, Efrosinja, wrote to Soviet officials in Kiev, to document that Viktor was wounded over Roslavl, allowing Viktor to receive a pension as a wounded veteran. [For a transcript of this letter, see Appendix C.]

yard, Anjuta, the younger daughter, saw me and my scorched appearance startled her. But when I spoke, she said, "I saw your plane burn and fall in the forest," and she brought me a bucket of water to drink. The daughter-in-law, Maria, came out of the cottage with her small child and, after I had drained the bucket of water, she and Anjuta helped me to the shade.

A joyful and tearful reunion in 1966 of Viktor with the Kuznetzov family, who saved Viktor's life after he parachuted from his burning plane over Roslavl.

Before long, Phillip and Anna came with vodka, some to drink, and some to pour over my wounds. For an injured man, vodka is useful both on the inside and the outside. With my broken ribs, breathing was painful. Philip bound my chest with a linen towel to ease the pain. Anna brought me food. The family laid out the plan, for I was not their first rescue. Phillip said that I must hide quickly, because certain Russians had defected to the Nazis, and these traitors frequently came to his house looking for airmen. Helping me along a hidden path, obscured by hummocks and overgrowth, Phillip brought me to his family's secret place, a hideaway that they had named "Burnt Bog." Here, evergreen boughs offered cool shelter. Every day, either Viktor or Basil brought food, herbs, and ointments to the hideaway. I was safe and being cared for by friends.

After about a week, I had grown stronger and could walk without assistance. At this time, Basil and Anton introduced me to two of their comrades who took me to their partisan camp, where I found several dozen men between the ages of fourteen and fifty. The atmosphere was friendly, I was immediately welcomed, and I was delighted to find there our co-pilot, Mashin, who had also found his way to this group. From the partisans, I learned that our pilot, Vihorev, had been saved by a different partisan group and had already got back to our own lines. Six of our crew who were trapped in the plane had perished, and the local inhabitants had buried them close to the site of the crash. Our navigator and air gunner had parachuted from the plane, but they were badly wounded and were not able to escape. Nazi soldiers found and shot them. Thus, of our crew of eleven, only three—Vihorev, Mashin, and myself—survived.

I was among brave friends. They told me of their activities against the German supply lines and they were eager to hear from Mashin and me how we were pushing back the enemy from the Soviet side of the front. There was no possibility of contact with their families, and we talked much of home. We exchanged names and addresses. As my wounds healed and my health returned, my spirits rose. Each day I increased the distance I could walk. Just a few steps beyond the camp took me into the forest, which was the densest I had ever seen. Unless one knew the way, it was impossible to move through it without an ax or saw. We were located near the Gabja River which flows eastward into the Desna. The nearest settlement was the village of Tjunino. This forest provided ideal concealment from the Nazis.

It was September, and summer had turned into the reds, oranges, and golds of a glorious autumn. Nature was impossible to ignore. The birds were migrating south, and sometimes I would come suddenly upon rare species—falcons and egrets. Even as I sat in the camp, the rookery of the forest sounded pleasantly in my ears. When I sat on the banks of the stream, beavers and ermine approached me fearlessly, and out of curiosity. Fish were plentiful, and I could catch them for dinner, even if my swollen hands could barely clean them. How sublime it would be to spend a summer along such a river; if I survived this war, I promised myself to do it. How could the world be so beautiful, I wondered, in the very midst of all this horror, misery and death?

But the business of war was always at hand and weighed heavily on me. These partisans were brave men, whose stories might never be told. When a band went out on a raid, I felt the same tension as at the radio station when our bombers were on a mission. Now, as then, some of our men did not survive. In the camp, I felt useless. The waiting was terrible; I longed to go with the partisans, even though I knew that I too might not survive.

As the swelling in my right hand gradually went down, I was able to hold and fire a pistol. I was assigned to a group of men from twenty to forty years in age. Our job was to harass the major German supply routes—the highway and railroad running from Warsaw. Our group was led by Lieutenant Sizov. In 1941, when his unit had become trapped by the enemy, he had slipped through the German lines and escaped. His prior military training had helped him become an expert in guerilla tactics. Throughout my career I have worked with many men, but I never found any more dedicated than those in our partisan group. "One can judge the flock by its priest"—the men trusted Sizov, and he, them. Without his skill and careful planning, our group would certainly have suffered more casualties than we did. If ever one of the men was wounded or killed, Sizov made sure we got him back to camp.

Viktor, standing second from left, with Soviet partisans in late autumn 1943. Although the partisans appear to be well outfitted for winter, their clothing had been borrowed for this photograph.

In autumn of 1943, during one of our night raids, we surprised and destroyed some enemy transports, but there was a fierce battle. Although we succeeded in capturing two German officers, the raid wasn't without cost, since one of our scouts, eighteen-year-old Vladimir Mashistov, received a fatal chest wound in the fight. Knowing that he would not survive, he asked me tearfully, if I were successful in crossing the front, to call on his mother in Moscow and tell her his story. Shortly after I gave him my promise, he became febrile and delirious. We buried him in a shallow forest grave dug with our knives and our hands.

For some weeks I had wanted to return to my own unit, and Mashistov's death increased this desire. Mashin also wanted to try crossing the front to return to our unit. We discussed this with Sizov, suggesting that, with the help of some of the partisans, we two could take the German prisoners, and try to cross over to our own lines. This would get the Germans out of the camp, and allow

Mashin and me to return to our bomber squadron, where we could be of greater use in the war. The danger, of course, was in getting safely across the front. In addition, those of our captured soldiers who did return from enemy territory were often considered to be traitors or spies and were imprisoned.[29] We hoped that having German officers with us as prisoners would demonstrate our loyalty. With the enemy retreating westward, we knew the front was now at the Desna River. Though winter was close at hand, the broad river was not yet frozen over, and getting across would not be easy.

Sizov agreed for us to make the attempt, and offered us the assistance of partisans who knew the terrain. Fortunately, the local men knew the locations of rapids and sandbars where we could cross the Desna River and the water would be only chest deep. So it was decided. Mashin and I, with the help of three partisans, Derjugin, Krotov, and Karpeshin, took the two prisoners and left the camp. We reached the Desna unobserved by the enemy. There was snow on the ground, but the river was not frozen over. We say: "If you don't know the ford, don't jump in." Now, it was really true. As promised, the partisans had brought us to a very broad but shallow section of the river. We each took off our clothes and folded them into a bundle. Holding these bundles and our pistols above our heads, and with our knives clenched between our teeth, we waded naked and silent into the freezing water. Numb with cold, but fortunately still undetected, we climbed out on the eastern bank and quietly slipped on our clothes.

We were now in no man's land in a boggy meadow between the two armies, with few trees to hide us. As we were moving eastward, German soldiers spotted our group of seven and opened fire with mortars, each shell raising a geyser of mud and water. Running as fast as we could through this swamp, sometimes from one shell hole to the next, we successfully approached our lines. Not knowing who we were, our own soldiers began to fire on us. We shouted out,

29 In *Gulag Archipelago.* Solzhenitsyn writes compellingly of how badly the Soviet Union treated its soldiers who had escaped from German captivity.

"Don't shoot, we are partisans!" Then we heard cursing in Russian, and a loud cry of, "Okay, you bastards! Who in the hell are you?" Never had cursing sounded so much like music. We advanced slowly and were recognized. A soldier took charge of our prisoners and escorted us to the commanding officer for debriefing. The commanding officer thanked us for delivering the prisoners, made sure we were fed, and then put Mashin and me on the train to Moscow.

When we arrived at our airdrome, we found that we had long since been listed as "killed in action." Once more we enjoyed a riotous greeting from our comrades. It was a wonder they could recognize us, considering the beards we had grown. Since falling from the airplane, my eyes had remained as red as a rabbit's, so I spent some days in the hospital under treatment. Subsequently, Mashin and I were assigned to the First Air Squadron of the 362nd Air Regiment where, for a few weeks, I flew on a transport aircraft.

Early in 1944, we were retrained to fly on a twin-engine bomber, the North American B-25J, which was part of the military aid supplied from the United States to the Soviet Union.[30] It carried a crew of six and was the best fighting machine I ever flew on. Other airmen who had no such airplane were extremely envious of us. We began combat missions again. Throughout 1944 and until the war ended in 1945, our targets were seaports in the Baltic region, including Kaliningrad, Pillau, Riga, Grossgaidekrug, Gdansk, Gdinya, Lipaja, Tilzit, and Klaipeda. We also flew missions to Budapest and Berlin. During one of the many fierce battles, my fellow crewmembers, Boldirev and Lukichjov, were killed before my very eyes.

30 In the years 1944-45, the United States Lend-Lease Program supplied the Soviet Union with thousands of planes, many being B-25 bombers.

Viktor, far left, with some of the crew of a Soviet Lisunov type 2 (Li-2) aircraft, which was the Russian version of the DC-3, built under a 1938 American license (aircraft identification by AFHRA, courtesy of Lt. S. Lopez). Igor Fomin (see Note3 Chapter 13) is pictured far right.

The B-25 had two 50-caliber "Colt-Browning" machine guns, which I used to good effect against German fighter planes. On one mission in 1945, when I was flying as a gunner and a radio operator, we had not been able to find our target in the bad weather. On the way back to our base, we saw below us a German military train en route to the front. We demolished it by dropping bombs on the front and rear of the train, but, as it was daylight, two German Focke-Wulf fighter planes spotted us and began to attack. As the first member of the crew to see them, I asked the captain to perform a complicated maneuver which would put them in my line of fire. Using the machine guns from the tail position, I shot down the first fighter. The other fighter plane flew away. In recognition of this, I was awarded the "Order of the Red Star." Between the 16th and 26th of April we flew four more missions over Berlin. My last combat mission was to bomb the submarine base in Swinemunde on the 30 th of April 1945, only days before our victory.

It was such a terrible war and no one wanted to die. I was lucky—I survived.

War be damned!

Berlin fell on the 1st of May 1945, and on the morning of the 2nd, the victory was announced. When we heard the news that Germany had surrendered unconditionally, we jumped out of our barracks in Baranovichi, embraced and kissed one another, wept for joy, and yelled at the top of our voices. In our own salute of victory, we ran to the airfield, climbed into our planes, and fired our 50-caliber machine guns into the air.

On the 8th of May, by order of the Supreme Commander-in-Chief, we were transferred to the base in Moscow. The next morning, when the surrender was officially announced to the Soviet people, I was in Red Square, where the mood of the people was jubilant. We combat soldiers were all embraced, kissed, and twirled around by the celebrating population of Moscow. As first-class warriors, we were granted the great honor of participating in the "Salute to Victory" that afternoon. Flying at only 2,000 feet above Moscow, we shot multicolored rockets and tracers into the air. It was an extraordinary display!

Later, dressed in our best regimental uniforms and wearing all our battle ribbons, three of us, Nick Chernolih, our navigator, Gregory Yaglov, our captain, and myself, went to the center of the city, where we were again greeted as heroes by all the people. We were treated to a torrent of adulation; we were tossed into the air and caught again, while the crowd cheered wildly. Everyone laughed and cried together and toasted each other with ale. By the evening, tired and needing to rest, we passed by the Bolshoi Theatre where *Swan Lake* was to be performed. We wanted more than anything to see the ballet, but there was a huge crowd at the box office, with majors and colonels and others who out-ranked us waiting their turn. Our hopes sank. But Chernolih, a junior lieutenant, was undaunted. Squeezing his way to the box office through the crowd, he called out, "Three tickets for Heroes of the Soviet Union!" Immediately the tickets were given to him. So it was that we happened to be at the Bolshoi Theatre on the evening of May 9th, 1945, along with Moscow's elite and the cream of international society, including Lady Churchill. The performance was wonderful!

For the next three days, we were given passes to Moscow. Although this was a time of fantastic celebration, I had made a solemn promise to Vladimir Mashistov and had a somber duty to discharge. On the 10th, I visited his mother at 2 Meschanska Street. At first, I told her only that I brought greetings from Vladimir. In a flash the news of my arrival spread, and soon all the women in the building came running to her apartment. There were no young men in Moscow at that time—only old men, women, and children. The women brought what they could for me to eat and drink and asked me about life at the front. I spoke truthfully about the war and, at length, told Vladimir's mother of her son's death. She began to sob uncontrollably, and then she fainted. We brought her around with water and smelling salts, but we could not console her. Those days of great victory were also days of great loss. I left those women with tears in my eyes.

Viktor P. Kramchaninov

10

The War: A Young Woman's View

Maria Rudenko-Kramchaninova

Now this cursed war is on us.
'Tis a wicked thing, God knows:
Where there should have been a wedding
To the war the bridegroom goes!

From *The Pedlars* by Nikolai Nekrasov (1821-1878)[31]

א

In 1939, the USSR and Nazi Germany signed an agreement that divided Poland between Germany and the Soviet Union. The southern part of what had been eastern Poland, including the city of L'viv, became western Ukraine. I had no appreciation of the coming disaster, but my parents and many others were worried. For years, our government had said repeatedly that the Nazis were fascists, and were enemies of Communism. So when the report of the August Non-Aggression Treaty between the Soviet government and Nazi Germany was made known, people could not understand it.[32] It was lightning from a clear sky. When Poland was

31 Published in English translation by Soskice (1977, p91).

32 The war between Germany and the Soviet Union was delayed by the infamous 'Non-Aggression Pact' (with its "Secret Additional Protocol", Appendix A) of August 1939 between Stalin and Hitler. The Pact assured that Hitler's armies could invade Poland without interference from the Soviet Union, which, in return, would receive a large slice of Polish territory, including the city of L'viv.

divided between Germany and the Soviet Union in September, this was also hard to understand. At that time, our people were told by the government that "our brothers in Western Ukraine" would be "released from bourgeois oppression." Only a few knew the truth. It was very dangerous to discuss one's doubts. From the peasants and upward, to our highest local officials, one heard only, "We are simple people; our chiefs know better. If we are not informed about something, then it is not necessary to inform us." We believed what was published in *Pravda*, and many things were hidden from us.

In September 1939, the Soviet government assigned my father, Pavel, to L'viv, where he was to be head of construction. For a person who was not a member of the Communist Party to be given such an important job was unusual. Father had completed only four years at primary school, and had received only half a year of formal training in construction, but he was self-taught, bright, and enterprising. I think the Soviet government had liked Father's work in Zhitomyr, and had an urgent need to assume control of the newly-acquired territory. In L'viv, he was assigned the supervision of eleven Polish engineers, all of whom had been well educated in Western Europe. He liked them and they worked well together, but Father's new assignment meant he must leave immediately for L'viv. Mother, Galina, and I stayed behind in Zhitomyr until I finished high school.

In May 1940, Father drove a truck from L'viv to attend my high-school graduation. The graduation party was a great success, and as Father played fiddle for the dancing, he enjoyed it immensely. But after the graduation and party were over, he had us pack our belongings into the truck for the journey to L'viv. It was to be only the beginning of my sorrows. Even after more than sixty years, I remember how hard it was for me to part with Viktor and our friends. Viktor and I thought we would soon visit each other, but fate ruled differently.

Pavel and Christine Rudenko in a portrait taken in L'viv on 6 June 1941, just sixteen days before the German invasion of Ukraine.

In the autumn, I began to study at the Medical Institute in L'viv. It was hard, because the medical subjects were taught in Polish, which was the nationality of the faculty. Only the Lenin-Marxist philosophy was taught in Russian. Many of the students, however, were now from Ukrainian families, and mass meetings were organized in the central courtyard, where students standing on boxes, barrels, or even trash cans demanded that all courses be taught in Ukrainian. As things gradually settled down, I became more interested in medicine, and I began to study hard. Viktor and I corresponded regularly.

While I studied medicine and thought of Viktor, my parents worried about the German army being just across the border, so close to L'viv. It was their greatest anxiety. The older people knew the costs of war with Germany, for they had not forgotten what it had been like in 1914. My parents could only discuss this in the lowest tones, and only between themselves or with their closest friends. Whenever there was a public meeting, someone would ask: "Tell us, will there be war with Germany?" The local Party leaders invariably answered: "Our government has ensured peace with Germany." Applause always followed. While I did not think about these things, my parents did. As if to provide a record in case of separation by war, they sat for a portrait in June 1941, only sixteen days before the German invasion. It was their only formal photograph. Their fears were well founded; our tranquility was not to last.

Soon after dawn on 22 June 1941, we heard the roar of airplanes, and saw them wheeling and circling at different altitudes like autumn leaves. At first, we thought it was a training exercise, until anti-aircraft guns began to fire and bombs began to fall, some exploding close to our house. Suddenly realizing that this was war, the people of L'viv rushed in panic to their basements. The city erupted into military activity. Cars filled with soldiers sped along the streets, and detachments of civilians with rifles, machine guns, and gas masks appeared. We saw tanks positioned on the outskirts of the city. Although we were told by the radio that the Soviet Army was in retreat, we were reassured that this was a temporary situation, and that the enemy would soon be expelled from our Motherland. Many people believed these reports, and only evacuated their families to nearby villages. Father had been ordered to continue his work, and so we also moved to a village nearby, where it was quieter and he could still commute to L'viv. But soon the order came to evacuate all equipment from the factories in the city, together with all foodstuffs and livestock. Within a few days, the war had come to L'viv. When fighting began in the streets, Father escaped by foot back to our village. There were no cars. He put us all in a cart and we headed for the railway station. We left nearly everything behind, although we did bring the family photo album. I also brought my medical school records, and for some reason, the gramophone. Maybe I was hoping Viktor and I could dance to its music again someday. I marvel now at how easy it was to leave so much behind, and at how one decides what to keep. At the railroad station, each family was given a document with a destination for the evacuation. We were to go to Lubni in the Poltava region, where Father had once been employed. But there were no trains. We had to travel by road in our cart. For the whole journey, I clutched my gramophone.

Fear has big eyes. Tractors, tanks, and carts choked the road. Most terrifying were the falling bombs from German planes flying overhead, while we in our cart were barely able to move. Bombs make no distinction between animals or people, civilians or soldiers, able-bodied or wounded, men or women, children or adults. Carts and tractors were bombed as readily as tanks or military cars. In this congested mass were terrified cows, horses, and sheep, and they too were hit by the bombs. I remember particularly the suffering of the wounded men as they bumped along on the two-wheeled carts. Only when we got far enough away to find a train and were able to go farther east did we become more calm. These horrors of war have stuck in my memory ever since.

In the city of Lubni, we managed to rent an apartment, which the owners had vacated when they left for Russia. Father found a job in construction, my sister found work as a bookkeeper at a cloth factory, and I became a laboratory assistant at a bakery. Father, now forty-six, was summoned to appear at the enlistment office for military service but, within a few days, he had returned to continue his construction work.

One morning, at the beginning of September 1941, I was on my way to work as usual. But something was terribly wrong. Trucks filled with wounded men were hurriedly leaving the hospitals, and other wounded were being carried to the railway station on carts and tractors. Horse-drawn sledges carrying the wounded were dragged over the cobblestones. Soon the sound of gunfire was heard from the nearby Sula River. Looking out from the window of the bakery, I saw a tank with a swastika on its side roll into the Market Square and fire its cannon down the road our soldiers had just taken. Some of our men fell and others dived into the ditches beside the road. We all ran home as the bombing began, and everyone hurried to their basements.

In the morning, when we looked out of our windows, the streets were full of German soldiers. Already, the Germans had posted up notices ordering all males to register at the commandant's office. People were afraid to leave their homes but their food supplies soon ran out. Some went to nearby villages to exchange clothes for food. After a few weeks, the German authorities ordered all Jews to assemble at the Market Square, along with their valuables and enough food to last them for three days. What a terrible and tragic sight. Despite the threat of death, some Gentiles hid Jews in their own homes. Some Jews hid themselves in cellars, but the Nazis found and shot them. Those who had assembled in the square were taken to a ravine outside the town where they were shot—old men, children, babies, and women—every one of them. All night long the firing was heard. None of us will ever forget.

The next disaster came a few days later. The Nazis began to round up the young people for forced labor in Germany. Young men and women were loaded like cattle onto the trains and shipped out. When I and my sister Galina, a year younger than myself, received our subpoenas to appear before the medical commission prior to transport, we decided on a medical ruse. I would become tubercular. Taking sputum from a patient who really did have tuberculosis, I smeared it onto a microscope slide and then applied the appropriate stain to demonstrate the tuberculosis germ. After writing my own name on the slide, I presented myself and my evidence to the commission. It was a risky thing to do, for had I been found out I would have been shot. But I could not think of another way out. After looking at the slide, the German physician even disdained to examine me, and he let me go.

We prevailed upon a local physician, who was an eye specialist, to help Galina feign eye disease. He admitted her to the hospital and each day, for several weeks, he dripped atropine into her eyes and kept them covered with bandages. She, too, was excused by the commission on medical grounds. In this way, we escaped being slave laborers for the Nazis, a fate suffered by literally millions of other Ukrainians.

Near the end of 1943, when the Soviet Army retook Lubni, we were released from German occupation. My parents had always dreamed that Galina and I would receive higher education and they did everything in their power to make this happen. Now that Lubni had been liberated, Father immediately began to search for work that would pay enough for Galina and me to attend a university. We would have to go to another city, because there was no institute of higher learning in Lubni. Since I had studied at the L'viv Medical Institute and had fled L'viv with my student card and record book, I could show the courses I had taken and my grades. In 1944, I presented these documents to the Kiev Medical Institute, and was accepted as a student in the pediatric faculty. I had to begin all over again and retake everything I had studied before the war.

The war had destroyed many houses and apartments in Kiev, so the Institute administration could not provide student accommodation for those with no family in the city. We had to rent a place where we could sleep, prepare food, and study—even if it was just a corner of an apartment. Luckily, soon after I arrived in Kiev, I met a very fine and modest classmate called Ludmila who was in the same situation as myself. We immediately liked each other and decided to share rent for a single room we had found. We saved money and could study better there than in a corner of someone else's apartment. We got along well and learned to eat economically, but our studies at the Institute were demanding. Just to keep up, we spent virtually all our time doing homework, writing summaries of the lectures and assignments, drawing the diagrams, observing and performing dissections at the anatomy laboratory, going to the library, and attending the scientific conferences organized by the students' society. Whenever there was a little free time, we hurried to the theatre. Running rather than walking, we arrived early enough to buy the cheapest tickets for standing room in the gallery, for any seats were far beyond our means. If we managed to buy tickets, we were like children who had been given a gift. After the performance we would discuss everything we had seen and heard.

Of course, after our family fled L'viv in 1941, I lost all contact with Viktor. I knew that he was fighting somewhere, but I had no idea where, or even whether he was alive. I wrote letters to his family in Zhitomyr, but they could not help, for they were also under German occupation and no communication was possible from occupied Ukraine to the Soviet Union. At the end of 1943, immediately upon hearing that Zhitomyr had been liberated, I wrote to them again, and they received my letter after the New Year, just before Alexander left to join the Soviet Army. Alexander, believing that he, being in the military himself, could better locate Viktor, took my letter with him. But when Viktor was given a short military leave early in 1944 to visit his family in Zhitomyr, he and Alexander missed each other. My precious letter had gone to war! Viktor's family did not have my address, and it took until June for Viktor to learn where I was living. On 7 July 1944, I received my first news from him. The little paper triangle, dated 30 June 1944, gave only his return address, Field Post Office 13730, on the one side, and a censor's stamp of approval on the other. But now I knew he was alive! My joy and relief knew no bounds. I answered immediately. Despite the war, mail got through. On 5 August, I received a second letter from him. The letter began:

> *How are you, Maria?*
>
> *Today I received the letter for which I have been waiting all these years. It has made me unspeakably glad! Although I don't know what remains within me of Viktor the tenth-grade boy, whom you last saw four years ago at the graduation party, a soft spot for you has remained in my soul. Wherever I went—everywhere—your photo was always with me, in the breast pocket of my army shirt.*

The letter continued with descriptions of what had happened to him in the battles he had fought. From then on, even though we had no envelopes or proper writing paper, we wrote on whatever we had, even newspaper or pages torn out of books. Folded into a triangle, unsealed and without postage, such letters went back and forth between us. Because of the war, they were not delivered as promptly as we would have liked.

Sample letter front and back from Viktor to Maria. Paper folded into a triangle, without seal or postage, served as wartime mail in the Soviet Union. Multiple postmaster stamps indicate the letter's torturous route.

29 September 1944

My dear Maria, Good Day!

I have not written before now because I have only just received your letters.

The battle goes on and we are pushing the enemy further and further to the west. Now we are delivering—right into the den of the enemy, Germany, and its ally Hungary—tons and tons of Soviet messages filled with the revenge of our people. We flew above Budapest to bring this last of our enemy's allies to reason; it is time for that scum to follow their neighbor Rumania out of the war. Now and then we have a hard time of it. But, as you can see, my Lucky Star guards me in combat; I am still alive, safe and sound, though I have had many close calls…

Maria, you asked me to send you a photograph of myself. It is enclosed. Some time ago, a military reporter for a newspaper visited us at the front and took this picture.

I have received a letter from Alexander. He is already out of the hospital and is again in combat on the front line in Lithuania. He sends you his best wishes. I wrote him a very severe letter, you know! He was in a hospital very close to me, but he wrote only after he had been discharged. I could have visited him! It was my dream to see him; we have not seen each other for four years! But I cannot be too hard on him; he is as solid as a rock, and a brave soldier in combat.

Maria, please write to me more often. Let me make myself clear: I very much want to see you in person, not just in a photograph.

How are you getting along at the Institute? Give my best wishes to all your family.

Kisses,
Viktor

Viktor, far right, with other crewmembers, including the pilot Gregory Yaglov (sitting next to Viktor), after a mission in 1944. On the back of the photograph, Viktor had inscribed, "Sorry to send you such a sour mug, but our job is not always fun."

With what ecstasy I read Viktor's letters from the front! Ludmila rejoiced with me. We reread them several times each day. When a letter arrived, I felt myself to be the happiest girl in the world. I was infinitely glad that he was alive and that he was able to write to me under the conditions of battle. Within the limits set by the censors, he told me the latest news of his air squadron. What I treasured most was his honesty in divulging his innermost thoughts and feelings. These triangles with the return address "Field Mail 13730" were so dear to me! It seemed to me that I had grown the wings of an angel; I did not walk on the ground, but flew through the air. When I received a letter from Viktor, the entire world seemed to join me in celebration.

Unfortunately, the joy of knowing Viktor was alive and the happy prospect of my getting a medical degree did not protect me from the illness that happened at this time. During the war years, many villages were emptied of able-bodied workers, and students were sent to the countryside to help with the harvests. In the autumn of 1944, students at our institute were assigned to harvest sugar beets on a collective farm. But there was no accommodation, and we had to live in a pigsty. It was dreadful, but we did our best to make it habitable. We spread around copious amounts of lime to improve the sanitation and the smell, and we layered the floor deep with hay and straw to provide our beds. But it was October, and autumn was far advanced. The walls had openings that passed for windows, but there was no glass in them, and at night the cold winds blew in upon us. During the day, machines were used to dig up the ground, but we had to use our own hands to scour through the dirt for the beets. Having gathered them, we sat upon piles of these tubers, preparing them for transport, while the cold rain drizzled down upon us. Temperatures fell, winds increased, and adequate clothing against the wind and rain were not available. We were always cold, both day and night. Many students fell sick, and I among them. I developed a high fever and a severely infected throat. In those days, penicillin was not available to treat my streptococcal throat infection. I was sent back to Kiev, and after ten days I was well enough to resume my studies. But then I developed acute rheumatic fever, which often follows strep throat, and which affected my joints so badly that for weeks I could hardly walk.

It was 1945 before I felt well again and was able to continue my studies. A letter from Viktor while I was recovering sent my spirits soaring. My sick heart was renewed by his constant love. Having told him of my illness, I needed and welcomed his encouragement to keep on with my medical studies. With this letter in my heart, I resolved to keep going—no matter what.

29 October 1944

Hi Marijka,

Well, there you go, you received my photo at last, and I'm glad of it. I think—I hope—that one fine day I will be able to return to you. It is going to get better; we just have to learn to wait. You probably don't realize that you are helping me to fight. Before every mission, it has become a habit of mine to take out your picture from the left pocket of my jacket where I keep it with my Communist card. I look at you and say: "Well, Marusia, where will we go today and what will we see?" And, together, we fly off to the war.

The time has long gone since, as a schoolboy, I dreamed about flying and thought of it as very romantic. Generally speaking, when the sun is shining and the weather is fine, it is very nice to fly over picturesque countryside, somewhere far from the front lines. But war, as you know, is not romantic. Fighting from the air, just as on the ground, is very hard work. It is physically hard—we sweat and sometimes we bleed—and morally it is even harder. Battle tests a man down to the very depths of his soul.

How am I? We are fighting and, I think, fighting well. For liberating the city and port of Riga, we received the Order of Gratitude from Stalin. Moscow saluted us. And now we are fighting heart and soul against East Prussia, the same place where the war started. And I tell you, Marusia, that German cities burn just as well as ours did not so long ago. At night, when we fly behind their lines, we can recognize Prussia from sixty miles away by the flames. The devil only knows what's happening on the front lines—but it must be some sort of hell.

How are you, Marusia? I'm so glad to hear about your medical achievements. It's true that this is something you must do; nothing else is as important for you now.

There is one question that worries me. We are not kids anymore, and I want to talk to you simply and honestly. Right now, in the midst of this war, it is very easy to make quick friendships, and you and I have many friends, both men and women, who are just that—only friends. I do not want to force you into anything but, if you value our feelings for one another, and if I personally mean a lot to you, please don't rush into some other relationship that you may later regret. Everything will come later for us, and I promise it will be legal and proper, as well as better and more beautiful than anything else. I often think about you, and not only as my best friend, but also as a woman, and as a girl I can share everything with. I don't mean that we should be prisoners and spend all our free time within our own four walls, but just that our friends should stay that—just friends.

I really like that lovely song "Marusia"—especially the words:

"For these two years, where 'ere I go,
Her picture to myself I show,
For two long years it has been so,
Maybe I'm a fool, but maybe no?"

I think, my dear Carrot-top, that you understand me. What do <u>*you*</u> *think?*

That's all for the moment. Best wishes to Galina and the old folks.

I hug you and hold you close to my heart,

Viktor

The time between one of Viktor's letters to the next seemed like an eternity. While I was recovering it was especially hard when there was no word from Viktor for a long period. The blackest ideas came into my head. I could not sleep; I could not study. Nothing pleased me: I was oblivious to everything that was going on around me. I wrote him letters again and again, and waited and waited. In my soul, I still had a glimmer of hope that he was alive. Let him be wounded if he must, but keep him alive! I hoped that we would survive this terrible time and, when it was all over, that we should see each other again. Now, as I look back on those days, I recall the poem by Konstantin Siminov:

WAIT FOR ME

Wait for me, I'm your tomorrow,
Wait though your strength be gone,
Wait through the yellow rains of sorrow,
Wait when the blizzard rages on.

Wait through Summer's heat and midnights dreary,
Wait though others have grown weary,
And forgotten yesteryear.

Those not steadfast, who let love abate,
How will they know, how understand,
Your waiting has saved me, preserved my fate,
From the fire of a burning land.
Only we will know that I live still
Because of your love and strength of will.
You alone, as no one else, did wait.[33]

And with what elation I received a new message from Viktor!

22 January 1945

Hello, my dear Marijka!

I have received your letter of 7 January, and I don't know how to thank you for it! I value it even more dearly than the others. I carry all of your letters in my pocket and read and reread them until they are just tatters and smudges. I have always kept you at the forefront of my mind and I know that you are waiting for me with all the strength and faithfulness that any girl could have. Maria, believe me, I will not fail to live up to your hopes. But both of us will have to wait till the end of this war.

For now, we continue to fight. We are advancing steadily and never before have we pressed the enemy as hard as we do now, right into the heart of East Prussia. I got a letter from Alexander and he is giving the fascists as hard a time on land as I am from the sky. He sends you his warmest regards and many good wishes. He sent me his photo—you know, his face has changed so much that I hardly recognized him. I had remembered him as the boy he was just before I left for the

33 Translated and rhymed by the editors.

front. Father is also in the army. Only the women are left at home now and they are waiting for us to bring victory. Now Berlin lies ahead, and the only way to you lies through it.

Maria, please write to me more often. Your letters are the only pleasures I have. I cannot hope to answer them all, but write all the same. Although it is now winter, it is sometimes very hot here. I am sending you my most recent photo. That's all for today. I wait for your letters and photograph. I want to be able to look at you every day.

Give my best wishes to the old folks, Galina and your girlfriends.

Kiss you and fold you in my arms,

Viktor

I kept each letter, and I still keep them, and I will keep them for as long as I live. I read and reread these yellowed triangles and endure our past all over again. In our youth, so many years ago, we trusted deeply in our ultimate victory over a heinous enemy, and this belief helped us to live through, and to struggle with, all of our difficulties. But now old age is upon me. The rheumatic fever I had during the war damaged my heart valves. Many other illnesses have come, and I must struggle with them daily. These old letters from Viktor help me get through the difficulties of my life today: difficulties which, in some ways, are not so different from those of the war years.

Maria Rudenko-Kramchaninova

11

Surviving German Occupation: A Boy's View

Gregory Kramchaninov, Viktor's younger brother

Up rose a black cloud like a wall
And reached for Heaven's gate,
And like the mother of all nights
It frowned with face of hate...

From *Moses* by Ivan Franko (1856-1916)[34]

א

In 1939 our family—my parents, Panteley and Barbara, my two older brothers, Viktor and Alexander, and myself—moved from Donbass to Zhitomyr. The cost of living was less expensive, but by autumn food was in short supply. As a growing eleven-year-old boy, I never got enough to eat, and the food available was low in calories, without meat or fat. There was even a shortage of bread. Each evening, a long queue appeared in front of the baker's shop, even though the shop opened at seven o'clock in the morning. Each person was permitted to buy only one two-pound loaf. People expressed their displeasure in whispers. If you complained aloud, the "black raven" secret police car would be at your door the next morning. Informers were in every queue. The food shortage was not because we failed to grow enough, but rather because trainloads of

34 Published in English translation by Andrusyshen and Kirkconnell (1963, p 243).

Ukrainian grain were sent daily to Germany, to satisfy the treaty signed in August 1939 between the German minister, von Ribbentrop, and our Molotov.

In 1940, Viktor left for the army, and my sister, Nina, was born. Because the food shortage was driving up prices, our parents decided to reduce expenses by moving the family from our house into a rented apartment. We found one in the suburbs of Zhitomyr, but for the five of us there were only three hundred square feet of living space—two small rooms and a kitchen. Somehow, we managed.

The summer of 1941 was very hot. One day, I went with Mother to the registry office in the center of Zhitomyr to get the special food allowance for families with many children. Bombs suddenly began to fall in the city, and we realized that war had begun. The date was 22 June. Our family had not expected a German invasion, so this was a dreadful shock. Soon, great numbers of people began to pass through our city as they fled to the east. These refugees told terrible stories, which together with the rapid enemy advance caused panic in Zhitomyr. What were we to do? Where should we run? We were paralyzed by fear and uncertainty.

Our parents first thought we should move east to the Donbass, where my sisters, Natalia and Katerina, lived with their families, but the war came too quickly. On 7 July, Father ran home from work and said that we must immediately evacuate to Kiev and that his factory had allotted a truck for our family. But then the offer was rescinded, because all transport was needed to carry wounded soldiers. We were told to go to the railway station, but the station was bombed even before we left home. Not knowing what to do, we stayed at home—no other option existed. The city officials distributed all food from the storehouses directly to the people to keep it from the enemy. Two days later, on 9 July 1941, only eighteen days after the war began, Nazi troops occupied Zhitomyr.

It was no longer living—only survival. Within a few days, Jews were ordered into a ghetto. The Nazis ordered all males between eighteen and sixty to register at the police office and at the labor registry office. Alexander, 15, and myself were exempted, for we were too young, but Father had to register, and I went with him. On the way, Nazi soldiers stopped us, claiming that Father was a saboteur responsible for an explosion near our house. In one of the most frightening experiences of my childhood, they were about to execute him, when, at the last moment, a Ukrainian policeman appeared and succeeded in stopping the execution. He was Father's good friend, whose old car Father had maintained in good condition for many months. He explained to the soldiers that Father was an honorable man, who could not have caused the explosion. Getting support from a policeman helped, but what made the real difference was the policeman's recommendation of Father as the best motor mechanic in the region. Father was released because the German soldiers knew that they would need someone to repair their cars, trucks, and tanks. Soon Nazi vehicles began to appear at Father's garage, and he was appointed to oversee other repair shops around the city.

The Nazis put up posters all around the city:

> *"Anyone who gives shelter to partisans, Jews, or prisoners of war will be shot!"*
> *"Anyone having a weapon, or a radio, or a subversive leaflet will be shot!"*
> *"Anyone who steals gasoline will be required to give blood—for each three ounces of gasoline we will take one half pint of blood!"*

Still, our family took many risks. We hid a few hens in a distant shed where they were safe from seizure. In the first few days, the German occupation was disorganized. Seeing the Nazi storage depots not carefully guarded, Alexander and I ignored the dangers and slipped in to steal food and anything useful. So, initially, we had food—some meat, potatoes, sour cabbage, cucumbers, cereals, flour, and fat—but soon such theft became too dangerous and we had to go into the forest to collect berries, mushrooms, fruits, acorns, and whatever else we could find.

With the help of one of his friends, Alexander was able to obtain a radio. He brought it home, hid it in the crawl space under our kitchen, and brought the antenna out onto the roof of our single-story house. Because discovery would mean death for the entire family, Mother covered the hatchway each day with sweepings, and disguised the antenna with laundry hung out to dry. Despite the risk, our family listened to *Radio Moscow*. It became our spiritual medicine and hope for forthcoming liberation.

Once, when searching through a bombed-out house, Alexander found portraits of the members of our Politburo. It was illegal to have such things, but we kept them as reminders of the past and hope for the future. One night, when we were looking at these, somebody knocked at our window. Mother quickly raked the photos into the ash pit. The knock was repeated. We opened the door to a well-dressed man about thirty years of age. He said, "I am a Polish Jew and I work as an interpreter at the Nazi office. Every day I wait to be sent to the Jewish ghetto, and I have decided to escape instead." He asked for worn, dirty clothes and to be allowed to stay for one night. Early the following morning, he went away. Such things happened often. Knowing our patriotism, neighbors frequently sent fugitives, especially soldiers, to our house. The risks were great, but we always helped them to escape: Mother could not refuse anyone in need.

Survival was the greatest challenge for everyone, but our family had an additional problem. We had to provide for my baby sister, Nina, who was a year old. How could we get her enough of the proper food? Mother made an agreement with a neighbor, who had a cow. In exchange for some of the milk, Alexander and I would feed the cow. And we did. We went to the forest with whatever tools we could find to cut grass and gathered sprigs that the cow might eat. We saved our vegetable wastes and scavenged those from other people. It was enough, for every day we got some milk for Nina.

Mother boiled foods like potatoes and carrots until they were soft. After these were finely mashed, she added breadcrumbs and made it all into a thin gruel which she carefully spooned into Nina's mouth, so as not to lose a drop. Nina seemed to understand, for she opened her little mouth wide, like a nestling bird waiting to be fed. After each spoonful, she would joyfully pump her tiny fists up and down.

Mother's resourcefulness was reflected in her motto: "God is God, but don't underestimate yourself." She was well known as a "jack-of-all-trades," sewing slippers, caps, jackets, and skirts. Father would bring home from the garage any worn out tires that had been discarded. With his help, Mother made shoes, using parts of the tire for the soles and other parts for the straps. She then exchanged these things for food in the market, in particular for curds and butter for Nina.

But how could we provide everything else an infant needed? As my parents were both busy, and because Alexander was now working with Father repairing engines, it fell to me to look after Nina, and I became her "nurse." Soon she was teething, and she began to walk by holding on to the furniture. She had curly blonde hair, big blue eyes, and chubby, dimpled cheeks. We loved her very much, and to us she was a little angel—a much-needed reminder that there was some good left in the world.

In the battles near Kiev, the Nazis captured thousands of Soviet soldiers. I remember how the Nazis drove these prisoners like cattle through the center of our city. Our men were ragged, dirty, barefooted, hungry, and bandaged. They were more dead than alive. When Mother saw them, she grabbed the cast-iron pot containing potatoes from the stove and ran towards the moving column of captives. Some of the other women also ran out with foodstuffs, but the German guards struck the women with rifle butts and shot any prisoner who reached for the food. Seeing what was happening, Mother cried out to the other women: "Throw the food on the road ahead of the prisoners—they will pick it up from there." And they did. As our men walked, they gathered food from underfoot, slipped it into their mouths and ate. It was an unforgettable, tragic sight. Many times during the occupation, Mother provided food in this manner to our captured men. Unfortunately, because of their treatment by the Nazis, few of those captured survived.[35]

There was always hunger, even for civilians. Now that Father was working in more than one garage repair shop, he earned a little extra money, and that helped. We also had Alexander's salary. Occasionally, I could help Father too, and for pay I was given a small loaf of bread, which I confess was pretty badly nibbled by the time I got home. In the spring, we planted a small vegetable garden on some land close to our building. It was not enough, so we ate acorns and the leafy tops of root vegetables. When Mother had a few moments to look after Nina, I rushed into the streets and prowled among the German military camps looking for scraps of food or anything that might be exchanged for it. No one had enough food for a normal existence.[36]

We had to resort to various tricks. It was dangerous, but almost every day we stole gas from German trucks under repair in one of the garages around the city, or we hid among parked Nazi vehicles to siphon off the gas. I carried the gasoline home in a flat flask fastened to my belly. Throughout the war, the skin around my navel was raw. Whenever we were successful in obtaining this life-giving liquid, we would bring it to the market to exchange it for food. Sometimes, with the money we got from selling the gas, Mother would go to the cattle market where she would buy the cheapest animal available, which always turned out to be a very old horse. Father would slaughter the animal. Some of the sausages we sold in the market. The risks were great, but we had meat! In the forest, we gathered acorns, dried them, and ground them into meal to make bread.

Alexander consistently took the greatest risks. Just before Christmas in 1941, at dusk on a cold day, a truck with canvas covering the load on its bed drove into the yard of Father's garage. The

---

35 Nazi brutality of captured soldiers quickly became apparent. Of the 600,000 Ukrainians taken prisoner in the 1941 Kiev encirclement, few survived the starvation, exposure, disease, beatings and mass execution (see Appendix D).

36 Inhumane treatment by the Nazis was not limited to prisoners of war but was also extended to the civilian population. [See Appendix E.]

driver and two German soldiers emerged from the cab and came into the office to warm themselves. The German guard at the gate also went inside to celebrate Christmas. The truck was now deserted and the yard unguarded. Alexander sauntered over and lifted the canvas to see what the truck carried. He saw bales of silk banners intended to decorate German army headquarters and official buildings. Quickly, he got into the driver's seat, started the engine, and sped to the outskirts of the city where he knew of a bombed-out building. He managed to hide all the bales in the basement. He then drove the truck to the opposite side of the city, where he left it on the street. He said nothing when he got home.

A great commotion broke out in the city. The Gestapo searched the garage, nearby houses, roads, and markets, but found nothing. After some days, Alexander surreptitiously brought home one of the banners, carefully hidden under his coat. The banner was made of heavy silk. The fringes were beautiful tassels, and these Mother unstitched and burned to ashes. She dyed the cloth a dark brown by boiling it for several hours in a broth made from onion peel and berries from elder and alder trees. When she had finished, no one could tell it had been a Nazi banner! She sewed a skirt from this material and exchanged it in the market for potatoes. That winter, Alexander made many dangerous excursions to his hiding place, each time bringing back two or three banners which, after Mother had converted them into clothing, bought potatoes, millet, soap, and kerosene at the market. It was a huge risk, but we survived!

By 1942, the front had passed far to the east, and Zhitomyr was deep in German-occupied territory. The Nazis imposed a strict and permanent curfew from 10:00 PM until 6:00 AM, but Alexander was intrepid. He was sometimes absent from home the whole night, and, during his absences, we heard explosions around the city. German storage depots, armored cars, and even the German commandant's office were blown up. The partisans were at work. Although we never spoke of it, we knew that Alexander had to be one of them. For each partisan demonstration of defiance, the German occupation forces reacted with bloody terror. They made unexpected forays into the market, rounding up innocent people as hostages. Some were shot or hung, while others were sent to work as slave laborers in Germany.

The Nazis had built a gallows for public executions in the city square. One day, after some explosions the previous night, German soldiers made a sweep of people in the market, and I was caught in their net. At gun point we were herded to the gallows, not knowing what would happen. When we got there, we saw that we were to be the unwilling spectators of the hangings, for they had already selected their victims. One was a teenaged girl with the rope around her neck. When she saw us, she cried out, "Long live the Motherland! Long live Stalin!" Immediately a soldier came forward. I will never forget the terror in her eyes as he kicked out the stool on which she stood.

For two and a half years, until the end of 1943, we were under occupation, living usually with hunger and always with fear. As we listened to broadcasts from Moscow on our hidden radio, we rejoiced at our victory at Kursk in the summer of 1943, and then again as our army recaptured Kharkiv in the autumn. We knew that the tide had turned against Germany, and we began to look forward to liberation. But the dangers were not over. Early in December, the Soviet army was advancing on Zhitomyr. In their desperation, the German forces tightened their hold on us. A patrol stopped Father and me on our way home from the garage. As usual, we had stolen some gasoline, which I was carrying in the flat flask on my belly. The German soldiers smelled gasoline and prepared to execute Father. At that moment, shells began exploding around us. We had come under heavy bombardment from our own army, which was now on the outskirts of the city. Once more, Father was saved from execution.

Zhitomyr was liberated, but only briefly, for the German Army soon retook the city. In a frenzy, German soldiers ransacked every house looking for men or boys to build defenses for them. For days, Father, Alexander and I hid in a narrow gully camouflaged with leaves. Only at night would we venture out, being careful to avoid

German patrols enforcing the curfew. When we were liberated permanently on 24 December 1943, we could finally return home.

After the liberation, Alexander joined the Soviet Army and fought with it right into Germany until the victory in the west. He was wounded twice, but both times returned to active duty. Father also joined the army. He was never wounded, but shells exploded near him on several occasions. Once an explosion covered him with dirt, and he was saved only because his friends quickly used shovels to dig him out. After the surrender of Germany in May 1945, Father, now fifty, was demobilized and returned home in June. When Viktor came home again on leave, we had a partial family reunion. Nina, a baby when Viktor joined the army, was now five years old. But there were two faces missing.

Absent was my oldest brother, Nikolai. He had joined the army in September 1941 and never completed his economics studies in Odessa. He became a company commander and was killed at Stalingrad in 1942. The government said only that he was missing in action, but an eyewitness told us how he died. He was hit directly by an incoming shell and disappeared in the explosion. The government never listed him as killed in action, and never awarded the family a pension for his military service.

Also missing was my brother, Alexander. After Germany's defeat, he was transferred to the Far East to fight against Japan. Later, we learned that he had been wounded twice in the lung and had died in a hospital in Voroshilov-Ussurijsk.[37] Of the five men in our family, only Father, Viktor, and myself survived.

37 The Soviet Union declared war against Japan on 8 August 1945 (two days after the United States had dropped an atomic bomb on Hiroshima) and invaded Manchuria on the ninth, also the date on which the United States dropped an atomic bomb on Nagasaki. Six days later Japan surrendered. Alexander must have been fatally wounded in the final days of World War II.

Post-war Kramchaninov family reunion, June 1945, in Zhitomyr. Front row, left to right: Panteley (Viktor's father, age fifty, who had just returned from fighting in Germany), Nina (Viktor's youngest sister, age five), Edik and Vadik (sons of Katerina), Barbara. Back row, left to right: Viktor on leave from the army, Katerina (Viktor's older sister), and Gregory (Viktor's younger brother).

After the war was over, life in Zhitomyr continued to be hard for several years. There was not enough to eat. Children would come to our house and ask Mother if she had something to give them, even if it was just enough bread to taste.

After I finished high school, I was fortunate to be accepted by an institute in L'viv, and Viktor and Maria kept the letter I wrote to them after I was admitted:

L'viv
25 August 1948

I hope you are well, my dear family in Kiev,

I received the letter from Viktor and Maria, which made me very glad. Now I report that I am enrolled in the L'viv Polytechnic Institute for Petroleum Engineering. I am very fortunate, for there were four or five persons applying for each place. In the entrance examinations, I did well in mathematics, but my brain swelled up during the English exam. As you may remember, in 1944 when I was in the ninth grade, we stopped studying German, and began English, so my only full year of English was in the tenth grade. But I forced myself through the exam as best I could, and somehow got admitted to the freshman class. Now I get the uniform free and 400 rubles a month! In five and a half years, I will graduate as an engineer. Viktor, I have a favor to ask of you. You remember the instruments you had in Zhitomyr? Here at the Institute, engineering drawing is very important, but for a compass I have only a sharp stylus with a pencil on the end of a string. If you still have your mechanical drawing kit, and don't need it, especially the compass, I could sure put it to good use.

Viktor, I know you have been angry with me for not pursuing my education. But I came here to L'viv to decide what my career should be, and now I have decided, and more than that have actually begun. This should make you very happy.

Regards,
Gregory

I married while a student at the Institute, and, after graduation, I worked as a petroleum engineer in the Soviet Union until retirement, save for two years in Afghanistan. My parents moved from Zhitomyr to L'viv. Father worked as a janitor, a job that was a waste of his marvelous talent for vehicle repair. In 1968, he became ill with prostate cancer and died. Mother then went to live with her youngest daughter, Nina, who by then was married to Viktor Drugov, an automotive engineer in L'viv.

Gregory Kramchaninov

12

Early Postwar Years and My Marriage to Viktor

Maria Rudenko-Kramchaninova

...it is not possible
for me to love another.

Marina to Dimitry from Boris Godunov by Alexander Pushkin (1799-1837)[38]

א

By 1945, I had recovered from rheumatic fever and returned to my studies. I ran about to clinics and libraries once again. Ludmila and I spent a lot of time looking for cheap foods and other necessities, but even with our scrimping, we did not have enough money. On some Saturdays we went for meals with my family in Lubni, and we returned to Kiev on Sundays. Sometimes my sister Galina visited us and brought from home some pies, meat, or bacon. We had won the war, but we still struggled with lack of food and too little money. All the same, we found time to go to the cinema, to museums, and to any new art exhibition. But during these difficult days, it was my correspondence with Viktor that buoyed my spirits.

38 Published in English translation by Barbour, 1953, and on the internet by Blackmask.com, 2002.

Then came a new crisis. Viktor wrote to me from a hospital bed. His suffering had not ended with the war—he had barely survived a third airplane crash!

Baranovichi
25 July 1945

Hello, my dear Maria!

We are used to sharing not only our joys, but also our misfortunes. I didn't want to alarm you before, but now that this terrible business is all over, I can finally write. On 17 June, three days after my visit to Zhitomyr, we flight-tested a new airplane. On take-off, we could not gain altitude and the right engine caught fire. We plowed through six utility poles and tore into a railroad embankment. The plane broke into splinters but, through some miracle, I survived. Nearby were some anti-aircraft gunners, and they dragged me unconscious from the debris before the fuel tanks and the ammunition exploded. None of the other five crew lived. Somehow, my Lucky Star is always with me when I'm on a plane. I had a narrow escape; I am covered with abrasions and bruises, my body is black and blue all over, and my hair and fingers are singed, but all this is a trifle. The main thing is that no bones are broken. Here in the hospital, they poke me with needles every day, but I am getting better and can already walk about. The guys from my squadron come to visit me often with berries and all sorts of small gifts, but the main thing is that they lift my spirits. I feel so sorry for the boys that died, especially Vladimir Astrahantsev. Do you remember him from my letters? I've often written about him. He was the one who had the cannonball slam in volleyball. Their remains, charred beyond recognition, are buried at the crash site. Soon I will be discharged from here and sent to a sanatorium in Crimea for convalescence.

You know, Maria, the Kiev Aircraft Administration has asked that I be sent there to work, and my unit commander has agreed, but it depends on the division commander. I will do my best to get the transfer. Why the hell do I fly on these coffins? I have had enough, though my friends tell me that after three crashes I will probably walk until I'm a hundred and crawl until I'm two hundred!

Don't worry about me! I'm okay. My best regards to your parents, and to Galina, and Katerina.

Write and tell me how you did on your examinations.

Kiss you with all my heart,
Viktor

Viktor's burns, though extensive, were not severe. He remained in the hospital for more than a month, and while he was there, as though he didn't have enough trouble, the political deputy searched his quarters. For the final year and a half of the war, Viktor had violated governmental regulations by keeping a diary, and it had gone undetected. Now the precious diary was discovered. Viktor was very angry that a petty Party hack, who had never faced enemy fire, should search his quarters and confiscate his diary. The war was over, and there were no longer enemy hands for the diary to fall into. The deputy brought official charges, but Viktor's military record may have saved him from prison, for he received only a reprimand. There was nothing he could do about his diary, but he felt bitter over its loss. In writing his memoirs, he often called upon his close friend, Sinitsa, whose diary had gone undiscovered. Viktor had no scars from the burns, but this third air crash and the loss of his diary scarred his soul for a long time.

After his discharge from the military hospital, Viktor was sent to the Livadia Sanatorium in Crimea. While there, he decided it would be possible to make a surprise visit to see me after he was released for return to his airbase. He would only need to make a short detour to Kiev en route from Crimea to Baranovichi. At that time, I was living in a rented apartment in the center of the city.

One morning, the doorbell rang. The landlady answered it, and then came and said that a military man was asking for me. As I had no military friends in Kiev at that time, the thought "Maybe it is Viktor!" flashed like lightning through my mind. My legs gave way, and my hands trembled so that I could hardly dress myself. When I went out and saw him, I threw my arms around him, laid my head on his breast, and wept tears of joy. We could hardly look at each other enough, and we could not believe our own happiness.

Viktor was no longer the embarrassed, confused youth I had seen six years ago standing in front of the tenth-grade class. Before me now was a slender military man with a courageous face and a very kind smile. While we were together, I was not on land; I was flying through the air! I felt like I had grown wings. I thanked God that He had saved Viktor through these terrible years. After we had settled down, we began to talk like wildfire about what had happened in our lives over the last five years.

We decided that we had to celebrate this joyous occasion. But what could a mere medical student provide? I decided to go to the General Service Department of my medical institute and take my food ration cards for the whole month. In exchange for them, I got a tin of stew, two pounds of halva (a sweet mixture of nuts and sunflower seeds), a tin of bacon and one of condensed milk. We went to the park and there had a feast, eating everything, while at the same time talking as fast as we could.

But reality is also harsh. The visit was short, for Viktor soon returned to his unit. He did not get the assignment to Kiev he had hoped for. Although he was retired from flying, he was assigned ground duty as the radio communication commander for a military division. However, we knew now that it would not be long before we were together again.

Viktor wrote of his plan for our reunion just before the New Year in 1947. By then my parents had moved to Kiev, and I was living with them. Viktor knew that major demobilization of the Soviet military was approaching, and that he would soon be released. It was time to plan our future, he said, and he asked me to come visit him in Balbasovo, a village near Orsha in Belorus, where his regiment was then stationed. Viktor's headquarters cooperated in his plan and put a car at our disposal. When I arrived at Balbasovo, Viktor met my train at the platform and we drove to his air base. En route, we decided to marry that very day. Our dream was to unite our lives in marriage for as long as we should live, and to live together in Zhitomyr or Kiev. We drove to Orsha thinking that we could register our marriage there, but, to our dismay, the only registry office was closed for repairs. What were we to do? We decided to go to any registry office we could find open. We found one in the nearby village of Baran, and there we were registered and received our marriage certificate. The date was 1 February 1947.

We returned through Orsha, where we had hoped to buy food for a wedding party, but we were disappointed. While we were being married, the open-air markets had closed because of the intense cold of -20 C (–4°F). All we could find was an insufficient amount of sauerkraut, potatoes, onions, and some very old meat. The men at Viktor's air base lived in dugouts because the buildings had been destroyed in the war. In Viktor's dugout, warmth came from an oil drum made into a stove. A door cut into the side of the drum received the wood to feed the fire. A pipe at the back carried the smoke out through the roof. On top of this oil drum we boiled the meat, sauerkraut, onions, and potatoes. We set a table, making everything look as festive as we could. When friends from Viktor's regiment came, they brought vodka. The party began! The men read poems that they had composed in our honor, we sang songs, and we danced to the *balalaika* until we dropped. It was a warm, heartfelt wedding reception, and no one complained that the food was poor and in short supply. The shared joy and friendship made up for the stark postwar surroundings. The next morning, Viktor put me on the train back to Kiev, and he returned to duty, though he would be able to visit me in Kiev from time to time.

Viktor wrote his parents that we were married, and his mother replied:[39]

---

39 Imperfections in Barbara's written language have been corrected by the Editors.

Zhitomyr
12 February 1947

Good Day Viktor

Today I got your letter. Congratulations on your marriage, and as your mother I give you both my blessings for a good future life. Somehow I have known for a long time that Maria would be my daughter-in-law, and I am happy that she is now your wife, for she is a fine girl. You will both need to study, and I know you will help one another. It is good that you will live in Kiev. Maria is so lucky to have a place there, because it is a great city for young people to live in. I am sure you will not forget us, even now that you are married. Maria and you will come to visit us, I hope. It is not too far from Kiev to Zhitomyr. As for us, we have no news to tell. Nothing here has really changed. I don't know why we have not had a letter from Alex. His silence bothers us a lot—we don't even know how he is.[40] *We received a letter from Natalia. Things are not so good for them, I'm afraid.*

We were pleased to hear about the demobilization. We now stock all kinds of seeds to plant in the garden.

That's all for now. Say hello to Maria from all of us.

Kisses,
Your Mama.

In May, four months after our marriage, Viktor was discharged from the army and came to Kiev. We could finally live together as a married couple. By not mentioning his 1945 plane crash to the medical examiners, Viktor was able to get a job as a civilian radio operator with Aeroflot. Between 1947 and 1953 he logged 4,000

40 One and a half years after the end of the war against Japan, Viktor's parents had still not been notified of Alexander's death on the far eastern front.

hours in the air. He said how absolutely delighted he was with this new sensation: "You fly, and nobody shoots at you."

Viktor and Maria Kramchaninov in May 1947, after Viktor was discharged from the army and had come to Kiev to live with Maria and her parents

We lived with my parents in a house in Kiev that Father had bought in 1946. In truth, it was only one wing of a house with two small rooms plus a smaller kitchen, but it had a garden and it was in the center of the city. It was convenient for Father's work, Viktor's job, the Medical Institute, and the libraries and theatres. Even though our housing was now better, the lack of food meant life was still hard. Agriculture and industry were stagnant, because war had destroyed thousands of Ukrainian villages. We were near starvation.

I became pregnant with my eldest child, Tatiana, but, having two years to go before graduation, I continued to study at the Medical Institute. During my pregnancy, my diet contained so little calcium and protein that two of my teeth simply crumbled. I was eating my own teeth to build bones for my child! On 30 December 1947, our medical class was observing a Cesarean section when suddenly my waters broke. The professor saw that I was in labor and immediately sent me to the maternity ward. Tatiana was born that day. I could only be with my baby for a month before I had to leave her each weekday to attend lectures and take examinations. Fortunately, Mother remained at home to look after Tatiana, and Father's job as a construction foreman was based in Kiev, so he was available to help. With Viktor traveling constantly and myself attending medical school, my mother, Christine and my father, Pavel, really became Tatiana's parents. Without their help, Viktor and I could not have managed.

In 1949, when I graduated in medicine, the presence of my parents at home became even more critical. As was usual with new graduates, the government assigned me to work, but in a rural clinic a hundred and twenty-five miles from Kiev. Poor bus connections and my schedule meant that visits home would only be possible occasionally on Sundays. Because Tatiana was just two years old, I objected to this assignment, but the Commission for Medical Assignment refused to listen. "It is your duty," they said, "to set a civic example for patriotism and to serve in this rural area."

The rural clinic provided prenatal, obstetrical, pediatric, and general adult care to seven villages with a total population of nearly ten thousand people. We had ten maternity beds. Our staff consisted of another physician beside myself and four *feldshers*[41] who could act as practical nurses, but there was no motor transport and we had only one horse. The horse and cart were needed to bring women in labor or other patients to the clinic, so I had to make any home visits on foot. Home visits, which have always been an important part of Soviet medicine, had to be made nearly every day. Some of the villages in our district were several miles from the clinic. When it was cold or snowing, I was glad to have Viktor's military fur boots and his fur flight jacket to wear. I was constantly near exhaustion.

41 *Feldsher* is the term used in many East European countries for a medical or surgical practitioner without full professional qualifications.

Viktor came to visit me as often as he could. Once, after I had been there for more than a year, Viktor came to visit, but I had gone several miles on foot to see a patient. The temperature was near freezing and it was raining hard, so Viktor decided to come after me. Rain had made the dirt road a soggy quagmire and Viktor struggled through mud over the tops of his boots. When he got to the village, he found me weak with exhaustion. He became very angry at the way the health authorities were treating me. They were requiring me to perform duties beyond my physical strength, and, besides, I had a young child at home. The next day, he went directly to the Minister of Health in Kiev. There he raised such a furor that I was transferred to the Kiev School for Blind Children, where I worked for thirty-five years until I retired.

There was a medical reason for my exhaustion. In 1944, the rheumatic fever had begun the slow progressive process of scarring my heart valves. I felt well while at rest and could easily perform light tasks, but I could not manage heavy work or prolonged exercise. In 1967, I had an operation by Dr. Nikolai Amosov,[42] our noted heart surgeon, to open a narrowed mitral valve at the inlet to the left ventricle in my heart. In the years since, the rheumatic damage to my mitral valve has continued, my aortic valve is leaking, and my heartbeat is irregular. Somehow, despite this heart trouble, I have managed to live all these years, taking care of my family and even working as a doctor. But now, as I write these words, I am always tired and short of breath.

Maria Rudenko-Kramchaninova

42 Nikolai Amosov (1913-2002), a dissident of the Soviet regime, was considered the "conscience of the epoch". In addition to an outstanding reputation as a cardiac surgeon, he is known for his book, *The Thoughts of the Heart.*

13

My Depression: An Aftermath of War and Hardship

Viktor Kramchaninov

New strength will relieve your tired heart of its load
The peace of your meadows restore you,
With pride you'll look back on your hazardous road
And joy will be lying before you.

From *Princess Volkhonskaya* by Nikolai Nekrasov (1821-1878)[43]

א

In the postwar years, I flew frequently with Aeroflot. While Maria was at medical school, Pavel and I were both working, but we still barely earned enough to feed our families. Tatiana had been born, so there were now five mouths to feed, and food was still scarce and expensive. My income from Aeroflot was necessary for survival, but the job was rather dull, because I was just using the radio communication skills I had learned in the military. In her letter of congratulation on our marriage, Mother had advised us to get more education. Maria was getting her medical degree, but my only education after high school had been as a military cadet. I wanted a degree in aeronautics, and the only way to get it was to go to night school while working my regular job.

43 Published in English translation by Soskice (1977, p60-61).

In 1947, I negotiated a deal with the All-Union Correspondence Electrotechnical Telecommunication Institute to become a specialist in wireless communication. By bringing a transcript of courses from the Moscow Institute to the Kiev Polytechnical Institute, I could study for credit in either city. So, after finishing my flights for the day in Moscow, I took evening classes there and did the same in Kiev. Between work and study, every night was taken up; there was no extra time, and the classes were not easy. I had never studied so hard. Although Maria now had our young child to care for and was working as a physician, she was a great help making drafts of my reports, writing abstracts, and typing up my examination papers. She helped even after our second daughter, Lena, was born. I finally graduated in 1952, but I didn't feel well. I was dogged by an unusual, disconcerting fatigue. The war, the work, the study, and the struggle to support my family finally took their toll and I became ill. I spent months in the hospital, and my illness continued after I was discharged. It was only because of the patient, persistent, and loving care of my dear Maria that I came through it. She always believed that I would recover, and she who got me back on my feet again.

One evening in the summer of 1953, after returning from a regular flight, I went to exercise at the gymnasium, as I often did. While there, I suddenly felt very weak and short of breath. An Aeroflot physician examined me and found a fast and irregular heartbeat. He sent me to the hospital where, after an examination and tests, the cardiologist, Professor Primak, diagnosed acute myocarditis—an inflammation of the heart muscle.[44] He told me that the only treatment was bed rest and that many patients do not recover. As he left my hospital room, he gave me a final warning: "Don't get up, or you will die!"

As a young man accustomed to enjoying the most robust health, this was a terrible shock. I feared for my life. I had survived the war,

---

44 Myocarditis, usually a viral inflammation of the heart muscle, can be fatal. In 1953 as today, bed rest is an important part of the treatment. However, because of his emotional depression, Viktor remained in bed long after his heart had recovered.

but now that I was on the threshold of a normal life with a wife, children, and a career, I was going to die. When one disaster comes up the path, you may as well open the gate, for more will follow. I lay in bed day after day, waiting for death to come. I was sure that every breath, every heartbeat would be my last. In the days and weeks that followed, the condition of my heart steadily improved, but no one could convince me of it, and my despair deepened. I had loved reading, but books no longer interested me. I had no appetite; I could not sleep. I lay awake most of the night, thinking the most depressing thoughts. Hope left me. When after some months, my mental health had not improved, the staff thought I might be better at home, and I was discharged from the hospital.

Though much that followed is a blur in my memory, Maria, who took over my care, remembers everything. At home, my mood was not better; I remained depressed, in bed, and aware of the slightest symptom. Once, on taking a few steps to the lavatory, I felt my heart beating strongly, and I lay down on the floor and demanded that the family lift me back into bed. I believed I would only get worse and could never get well. I feared the slightest interruptions, which became irritating annoyances. I refused to see friends when they visited, because they exasperated me. Even my children, whom I loved, became unbearable. I could not endure the sounds of airplanes, the usual noises from the street, or the conversations from the nearby room. I demanded that the curtains be drawn and the room be kept dark. I became self-absorbed, heeding only my own personal feelings and my symptoms and having no interest in my family or anything around me. When the psychiatrist, Professor Mankovsky, came, he advised that I be hospitalized for depression, but Maria refused, insisting there must be a better way.

Necessity made Maria unusually assertive. In our family, we say that the father is the head, but the mother is the neck, and she can turn the head as she pleases. Maria took on the job of turning me right around, head and all. Day after day, she urged me to get out of bed, but I was afraid. She persisted. One day, with me leaning heavily on her—for I refused to walk without support—we went out to the garden where I sat for a few minutes on a chair. After a few days, she devised a slight change in strategy. She took a glass of cold water and set it on a little bench a short distance from my garden chair. She pleaded with me to take one step on my own to the bench and to sit and drink the water. At first I was afraid, but one day I took the step, sat on the bench, and drank the water. I was surprised that it made me feel better. I had finally done something on my own. It was a day of triumph for Maria!

The next day I took the same step easily, but refused to take the second and only sat on the bench and drank the water. Maria never gave up. Every morning she had me take one or two steps on my own. Then she had me sit for a quarter of an hour while she bathed my feet in cold water. When I began to go into the garden more easily, she even had me walk barefoot on the wet asphalt. She hoped that any new stimulation would improve my emotional state. Little by little, I increased the time I spent in the garden, until I spent most of the day sitting under the tree or gathering apples and pears from the ground. But still, for a man who had been so active and vigorous, my progress was slow.

Maria felt that I was on the threshold of good health, and that further recovery lay in believing in my own strength. How to make this happen? While pondering what to do, she was told by a neighbor about a man named Grandpa Boguz. He was a folk healer who lived in the countryside away from Kiev. By reputation, he helped people suffering from depression, using hypnosis and suggestion, and without medication. Our government persecuted these healers who functioned outside of the state medical system, but they were popular with the people, and their fame spread by word of mouth. From what she had heard of Grandpa Boguz, Maria thought he was the very man I needed.

She wrote to him and took the train to his village. There she found his neat white thatched cottage, with a stream running nearby. Boguz himself answered the door. He had a broad face which emanated good humor and intelligence. Maria liked him immediately. He agreed to return to Kiev with her. On the train, Maria told him about my illness and everything she had done so far. He told her that he had experience of other men with similar problems, and that he believed he could help. His only requirement was to be left alone with me day and night until he had done what he could.

How well I remember when he first came into my room. I saw a strong, stocky man with broad shoulders, a thick gray beard, and a good-natured smile. Though he must have been at least sixty years of age, he was powerfully built and as agile as a man twenty years younger. What impressed me most was the sparkle of intelligence and kindness in his eyes. Boguz introduced himself—he spoke Ukrainian—and drew his chair up to my bedside. For the next fifteen minutes nothing was said, but somehow neither of us was embarrassed by the silence. At length, he spoke again. He proposed that, if I were agreeable, we would spend several days together, speaking or not, as we pleased. I asked if he thought he could make me well again. He waited to answer and regarded me with a steady gaze. Finally, he replied that I had within myself the power to get well, and that he would only show me that power. There was such confidence in this man, such strength in his quiet voice and kindness in his eyes, that I began to think it might just be true.

We began to talk, or rather I began to talk, in response to his questions about my life. Even though we had just met, it seemed as though we had known each other for a long time. As I talked, he watched me, listening intently and silently, with just a trace of a smile on his face. Sometimes I felt that I was speaking directly to those intelligent, kind eyes, and that they understood everything perfectly even before the words were out of my mouth. Never before had I found it so easy to talk to someone I had just met. Before I knew it, four hours had passed. He then asked Maria to bring in two glasses of vodka, each with a piece of bread. But when he proposed that I drink my glass of vodka, I became frightened. "Don't be afraid," he said, "while I am here no harm will come to you." Maybe it was the confidence that emanated from this old man, or maybe I was reminded of the war—of returning to the squadron dining room after a successful mission to find bread and vodka at each man's place. It had been a solemn celebration among comrades, of accomplishment, of success, of life. I followed Boguz's advice and ate and drank; and I felt strangely at peace. In that moment, I began to relax.

For the next week, whether in my room or in the garden, we were alone day and night. In all that time, he never offered advice, nor did he make any judgment about why I was ill. Each morning he would recite an inspiring poem or read a passage from literature to give me hope or strength. He kept telling me that I would recover. Then we would begin to talk about my life, starting with my earliest memories, and continuing through my youth, my experiences in the war, and all that had happened since. In telling him the details of my life, images arose that had long lain in the shadows of my memory. As we talked, these shadows became real. The memoirs that I now write have their roots in those talks with Boguz. Even though he is no longer alive, the memories now spill out onto the page as though I were talking to him. Hour after hour, we talked; Boguz asking questions, and listening with great care to the events of my life. He never interrupted, and there were frequently long silences. Occasionally, he would comment on how I, or some member of my family, had successfully dealt with crisis. During these days and nights, I came to understand myself and how many adversities I and my family had overcome.

We spoke much about the war. The memories were vivid. Even though my diary had been taken, just writing it had locked the details in my mind. Boguz understood everything. On one of the few occasions that he spoke about himself, he explained that what was happening to me, had happened to him. As a Bolshevik he had fought in the Civil War. He had seen and experienced the same horrors. His comrades had died in his arms, he himself had been wounded and, when the fighting was over, he had become depressed, just as I had. His own grandfather had helped him through his depression, had taught him hypnotism, and had shown him how to help others. Now helping others was what gave him the greatest pleasure. Through this old man I began to understand myself.

After a week, Grandpa Boguz announced that he had to return to his own home, and he suggested I come and visit him. I felt more confidence in myself, but I had not gone beyond our house. After two more weeks, I decided to go, and Maria went with me to the train. I was still afraid, even of the exertion needed to climb the steps up to the coach. I put one foot on the lower step, but Maria had to put her shoulders under me and push me up step by step into the carriage. All illness is in the mind.

I spent a month with Grandpa Boguz. We began each day with special prayers and poems. Together we read sermons offering hope, strength, and encouragement. With persuasion and hypnosis, he enticed me to walk with him through the tree-lined country lanes near his home. Knowing that I had done some fishing, Boguz really drew me into it. He kept a boat on the stream that flowed by his house, and he was an expert fisherman. At first we went out in the boat together, and then I would go alone for hours on end. Together we cooked the catch, for we did our own cooking; it was part of my treatment.

Boguz taught me how to make fish soup using his own special recipe. We divided the fish into three portions and removed the scales from the largest piece only. One portion was wrapped in gauze. We put celery, sliced carrot, onion, a bay leaf, salt, black pepper and peeled potato into a pot of boiling water and, when the potato was nearly done, we added the gauze-covered fish. After boiling the stew for several minutes, the contents of the gauze were discarded. We used the same gauze to wrap the other portion of fish and added this to the pot for a few minutes. Finally we added garlic, dill, other spices, and the largest portion of the fish meat—without scales or gauze. Then the kettle was covered with a lid and removed from the fire to cool. The soup, always accompanied by vodka, was aromatic and nourishing. Boguz warned that, if eaten at night, this soup prevented sleep, but I did not believe him. To convince me, we had it for supper late one evening. Just as Boguz had said, we were unable to sleep. Fortunately, there was a full moon that night, and we walked along the river and through the fields until nearly dawn. I am still curious why this soup has this stimulating effect.

By now, my strength and confidence had returned. Boguz felt that I had recovered sufficiently to return home. Maria came to fetch me, and when she arrived, I was out fishing in Boguz's boat, and he was reading beside the stream. I was proud to show Maria how well I felt, and I walked briskly to the train and jauntily clambered up the steps into the carriage. Our journey home was most pleasant. From then on, my strength and my spirits continued to improve. My illness had lasted for nearly two years.

By 1955, I was ready to work again. But where, and at what? A blacksmith makes horseshoes, and a frog catches flies from its pad, but what about a war veteran? For me, my "pad" was aviation; from it I had launched my career. My "horseshoe" was teaching; it had long been my passion. I had taught my brothers to play their musical instruments, my classmates their lessons in high school, new army recruits to handle weapons in Zhitomyr, and my fellow airmen to survive combat. I found my niche with the Ukrainian Civil Air Fleet, teaching pilots and air maintenance crews. It was the perfect job. In my teaching, I always tried to keep in mind four key points. First, to maintain a high standard for the students—the school at Charmotte and the Institutes in Moscow and Kiev had taught me that. Second, to maintain strict discipline—my parents and the military had drilled discipline into me. Third, to maintain humor in the classroom—high school in Zhitomyr had shown me that fun goes with learning. Fourth, to maintain a personal interest in my students—at high school in Zhitomyr, our "ragged-assed Europhile" had loved his students, and we worked hard to please him.

Viktor teaching aircraft maintenance at the Ukraine Civil Air Fleet's Institute for Advanced Training of Pilots.

For more than thirty years, until my retirement, I taught aircraft navigation and maintenance at the Institute for the Advanced Training of Pilots in Kiev. I worked at the Institute for such a long time that nearly all the pilots in Ukraine had become my friends. As the years went by, many of them sent me photographs of themselves with inscriptions on the back. Some said they remembered me for my humorous lectures, but I rather hope that they remember my two textbooks on air navigation and my insistence that they carefully learn the skills of their trade. Many letters indicated that I was a demanding teacher, and it was true. In 1944, Igor Fomin from our regiment had sent me his photograph inscribed, "In memory of our long friendship and to the best teacher I ever had. And even though he had to beat it into me, I don't hold that against him." Another photograph from March 1945 read: "To Viktor from Timoshin, a brother in the Riga Regiment. I give this photo to a model teacher, educator, and friend, who punished me often for my irreverent jokes and sharp comments."

My recovery was permanent; the depression did not recur. Grandpa Boguz always made light of his contribution, saying that he had only shown me the strength that was already within me. He accepted small gifts from us, but he would never accept money. Perhaps refusing payment lessened the chance that he would be targeted by our government, although it is strange that someone should be persecuted for helping others. Boguz derived pleasure from helping other people, and making someone well was his reward. I have always felt grateful to Boguz, but I would never have recovered had it not been for Maria's love and her constant care.

Viktor Kramchaninov

14

Family Life in a Changing Soviet Union

Tatiana Kramchaninova-Serebrovska, Viktor and Maria's daughter

Then shall our day of hope arrive,
Ukrainian glory shall revive, ...

From *The Epistle* by Taras Schevchenko (1814-1861)[45]

א

I was six years old when Father became ill, and seven when he came home from the hospital. My sister Lena was three. Sharing such a small space was not easy; Father occupied one room by himself, while the rest of us—my grandfather and grandmother, my mother Maria, Lena, and myself—crowded into the other room and the small kitchen. If I were ever to learn patience, which I am afraid I never did, I would have learned it then. There were now only two wage earners, Grandfather and Mother, so there was not enough money to feed six mouths. Just as she had during the famine while Pavel was in prison, my grandmother rose to the occasion. If she had a job to do, she did it herself—she never asked anyone to rake embers out of *her* fireplace. Her main duties were to care for the grandchildren and to buy the food, and she did both together. She always took me to the market with her, where she gave a virtuoso performance. Some of my earliest memories are of Grandmother

45 Published in English translation by Andrusyshen and Kirkconnell (1963, p136).

seeking out the least expensive products and arguing over every *kopeck*. She had perfected the art of queuing simultaneously in more than one line, for butter, flour, and sugar, and I would help her. Of course, this led to verbal battles in which the other women would shout, "You didn't stand in this queue!" When the items sought had almost sold out, the battles nearly became physical. Somehow, Grandmother managed to emerge unscathed and with the prized purchase. Her thriftiness saved us enough money that she was almost a third wage earner. I cannot imagine how the family could have managed without her.

When Father recovered from his illness and went back to work, even as a child, I could tell that life became easier. To start with, the five of us no longer had to sleep in one room and a kitchen. Father's health and employment improved his mood. Having a settled job in Kiev, he could spend nights at home with the family. Because he no longer flew, he could work fewer hours. Working at something he enjoyed made him happier, and having another wage earner relieved pressure on the family budget. We all felt a load had been lifted from us. Early in life, I learned how important it was to have a healthy father.

We still worried, Mother most of all, that Father might not stay well. Even though we could ill afford it, she insisted that he eat well, and have meat in his diet every day. It became my job each morning to buy three ounces of sausage for the sandwich Father took to work. The butcher cut the sausage into sandwich-sized pieces, and Father always counted these pieces when I got home. Sometimes the butcher had to include a small extra piece to make up the exact weight, and this was my reward. The sausage smelled so good that I always prayed for a little extra piece and when there was one, I happily sucked on it all the way home. Father stayed healthy; his illness did not recur. Some people believe in the healing power of chicken soup, but I believe in sausage.

By the age of eight, I was in second grade, when children were expected to join the Pioneers. Our class of forty students was divided into four squads and the leader of each squad reported to a

Council, which was part of a Pioneer detachment representing the whole school. The school, in turn, was linked through the Young Communist League to the District Committee of the Communist Party. It was a chain of command which put the Pioneers under tight Party control. We were taught obedience and discipline. We were taught to love the Motherland and the Party, which, as far as I could tell, were one and the same. There was always a special ceremony at induction, where everyone recited the oath of allegiance. Then we were given Pioneer badges and red ties. Model students were the first to be invited, and I fell into this category. Later, rowdy students and those with poor grades were allowed to join. My good grades must have gotten me in early, for my behavior was hardly a recommendation.

I was an unruly child. If some boy pulled my pigtails in class, I would punch him right then and there, and I was strong enough to do it. The teachers wrote criticisms in my grade book, which my parents had to read and sign. Once, after several particularly bad days at school, Grandmother Christine said to me, "Listen to the radio. They have just announced a broadcast about your school." Ever ingenious, Father had brought from work components with which he built a radio and then he had installed it in a large cabinet. As I listened to this radio, a few moments of music were followed by the deep, rich voice of the announcer. He said, "In School Number 48 there is one excellent pupil, but she is very badly-behaved. Her name is Tatiana Kramchaninova." Then he went on, "Tatiana, do you hear me?" Startled, I pressed my mouth close to the radio and cried into the loudspeaker, "Yes, yes, I do!" "Do you promise to be a disciplined Pioneer?" asked the announcer. "Yes, yes!" I screamed. Only some time later did Mother tell me that Father had connected a microphone to the radio and had spoken from another room, simulating the announcer's voice. Along with his other talents, he was a very good actor, and on that day he had convinced me. I had been shocked by what I believed to be public exposure of my bad behavior.

I tried to improve, but was not completely successful. Father needed to teach me the lesson more forcibly. It happened the first day of May that year, when Communist workers celebrate their international solidarity. Spring came early and warm, and the trees bloomed with all their strength. As was usual for this great celebration, the marching of troops and parading of workers would take place on Kiev's main thoroughfare, Kreschatik Street. Kiev is really a city of hills, and Kreschatik Street runs along the valley between two of them, Pechersk and Princely City. During the night, soldiers and police came in military trucks to partition off all the streets leading down these hills to Kreschatik Street. They built platforms for the audience along the parade route, and a special rostrum for Party leaders at the center. Early the next morning, workers with banners and flowers would gather at designated places on the hills to form columns for the march. People represented every workplace, factory, and school, and each column was led by a responsible Party official. This important holiday was strictly regulated by the authorities, and those admitted to the platforms were given special passes. Father always had a pass, and lifted Lena and me onto his shoulders, where we watched everything with delight.

On that morning, I wanted to see the people gather and learn how they formed themselves into columns. From my earliest childhood, I have always been adventurous. Without telling anyone, I took Lena, four, by the hand, and we sneaked out of the house and into the street. Knowing that passes were required for the staging areas, we waited until the soldiers were looking the other way and then we quickly slipped under the barricades. We soon found ourselves in the upper square where thousands of people were assembled. Patriotism from the Great War still prevailed in 1956, and everyone was in a festive mood. While people waited for instructions to move, they sang and danced. Everywhere we heard laughter and music. People warmed themselves with nips of vodka and ate whatever snacks they had brought with them. They were all poor, but they had dressed in their finest for the parade. Of course, in such a huge crowd, I soon got lost. It was several frightening hours, with Lena in tears and sobbing loudly, before I finally found my way back home. Having despaired of finding us in this human whirlpool,

Father had wisely waited at home, and he was enormously relieved to see us. The relief soon gave way to discipline, because he used his belt to encourage better behavior. I was a better Pioneer after that.

There were wonderful things about being a Pioneer. We were taught to love our country and to defend it, even to the death if necessary. This spirit had seen our country through the Great Patriotic War. As Pioneers, we all engaged in sports or the arts. At each school there were amateur arts performances, and groups which encouraged cultural or technical creativity. None of us loafed idly in the streets, for we were always kept busy. As Pioneers, we were taught to love our neighbors, to help the aged and sick, and to assist fellow students who were having trouble with their studies. Because of the Pioneers, there were no drifters in the countryside and no brigand gangs, the likes of which blossomed after *perestroika*.[46] In the summer, we went to Pioneer camps in the countryside, as Boy and Girl Scouts do in Western countries. We slept in tents and went on long marches, which made us hardy and more courageous. We studied nature, learned to kindle a fire, and worked together on clean-up details, which taught us to love the outdoors and work as a team.

Unfortunately, there were unpleasant aspects. What could have been wonderful was sometimes dreadful. We disliked the rigid requirements at the camps to march exactly and silently in line and to execute implicitly any command. Much worse were the Pioneer meetings, which we were required to attend and which we hated. At these meetings, our friends were put on trial for some real or imagined offense; they were publicly degraded and their very souls wrenched out. These "hearings" resembled a medieval inquisition with no tolerance of dissent. To this day, I remember them with embarrassment and distaste. They made us a compliant, gray army of children, devoid of initiative.

---

46 A partial definition of *Perestroika* by the USSR Party Plenum of 1987 was "the energetic liberation of society from the distortions of socialist morality" (http://www.anet.net/-upstart/perestro.html).

There was a schizophrenia in what the Party was teaching us. On the one hand, we were encouraged to be creative and to love our fellow human beings, while on the other hand, creativity was snuffed out and hatreds were encouraged. The Party wanted two contradictory things at once. Most confusing to my childish mind was the requirement to report all suspicions to the Party. Pavlik Morozov was held up to us as the classic example of a "Pioneer hero." The young Morozov, we were told, reported to the secret police that his father, a well-to-do peasant, opposed Soviet authority. Because of his son's denunciation, the father was arrested and killed. I was bewildered. I loved my family; why would I want them killed? When I told Father what I was being taught in the Pioneers, he was exceedingly disturbed. It was important to be loyal to the country, he said, but spying on people was a gross exaggeration of loyalty, and reporting one's family to the secret police was unthinkable. Party leaders must have thought that children would not appreciate the contradictions, yet inconsistency in adults is what children recognize most quickly.

Pioneers were required to collect recyclable items, especially scrap metal, and the schools competed in this. When our school went on an excursion to find scrap, Father often accompanied us. He took a lively interest in all of our activities. He once drove a truck containing some old surplus airplane components to our school. With this mass of metal we easily took first place in the competition. Father had great interest in the students, each of whom he knew by name, and, of course, he was very popular with them. On one occasion, he organized a field trip to his airdrome for our whole class, where every student got a helicopter ride around the airport. We were ecstatic! He was a natural teacher, and he discussed my lessons with me, but he never told me what or when to study.

As time passed, life became easier. We had enough to eat. Our family life became more stable. We were able to go to concerts, and to buy furniture—even a piano. Father organized an orchestra from among his colleagues at the airdrome, and they gave concerts of popular and semi-classical music. Although he could not read music, he conducted the orchestra, knowing all the parts by memory. As life improved, we worried less about survival and thought more about education and culture.

More and more, I began to appreciate a healthy Viktor. He was a wonderful father, who taught me to love the subtleties of nature. In summer, he took Lena and me to the Dnieper River to walk along its steep banks, where the beautiful forest parks stretched for miles. He taught us about the forest plants and trees, especially the mushrooms. He taught us about the fish—their names, their habits, how to catch and clean them and, of course, how to make his specialty fish soup.

I remember the bright, colorful days of autumn, when the yellow and red leaves from the chestnuts and maples had fallen and had been raked into huge heaps. Father tossed us onto these piles. We buried ourselves with screams of rapture and were as happy as puppies! On these walks, he taught us poems, for he knew a great many by heart. It was Father, not my school teachers, who taught me the poems that I still remember. A favorite from these walks were some lines by Shevchenko:

The heart grows warm to see it plain,
The village in our own Ukraine—
As gay as any Easter egg;
Bright groves of green its borders peg;
The orchards bloom, the cots are white,
The landlord's halls the hills delight,
A house of wonder; all around
The broad-leafed poplar-trees are found;
Then endless fields and woods o'erspread
Blue hills beyond the Dnieper's bed;
God hovers there—one might have said.[47]

47 From the poem Kniazhna (The Princess), part of Schevchenko's autobiographical verse, as published in English translation by Andrusyshen and Kirkconnell (1963, p89).

He also taught us poems by Pushkin, Lermontov, and Nekrasov. Those were wonderful days!

I must have learned to behave in school, because in 1962, when I was in the ninth grade, my teacher called me aside and privately loaned me a small, well-worn, paperback book. She simply said that it was something that I might like to read. It was Alexander Solzhenitsyn's short novel *One Day in the Life of Ivan Denisovich*, which the General Secretary of the Party, Nikita Khrushchev, had authorized for publication that year. It was part of his campaign to discredit Stalin.[48] The novel described life in a Siberian prison camp like the one where Solzhenitsyn had spent several years. The book was an immediate sensation. Persecution had been so widespread within Soviet society that the book touched a sensitive nerve within nearly every citizen, but with the memory of Stalin so recent, fear of reprisal prevented open discussion. Father also read the book, but he handed it back without comment. It may have impressed him subconsciously, for later he avidly read Solzhenitsyn, but for now he was not ready to accuse Stalin. Furthermore, the "Khrushchev Thaw" was brief. Khrushchev was ousted in 1964 and replaced by the more conservative Leonid Brezhnev, who initiated a wave of arrests of Ukrainian intelligentsia. My teacher escaped censure, and Father held his peace.

As our lives improved, so did our holidays. The most important were New Year's Day, the first of May, Victory Day on May 9, and the day of the Great October Socialist Revolution. Year by year, celebration of the favorite holidays—Victory Day and New Year's Day—became less public and more private. People still went to see the great victory parade but, afterwards, they celebrated in their own homes. In our family, we always had a grand meal and many guests. Each of us prepared for the celebration with great anticipation. We did amateur performances, recited verses, told stories, and

48 Alexander Solzhenitsyn (1918-) was imprisoned for eight years in 1945 for writing to a friend a letter critical of Stalin. After his release he wrote 'One Day in the Life of Ivan Denisovich', which was based on his own prison experiences. In 1970 he received the Nobel Prize for literature.

sang Russian and Ukrainian songs in four- or five-part voices. Of course, Father and Mother were the organizers and the center of attention on these occasions.

The Soviet government officially declared Christmas Day and Easter Sunday as "All-Union Communists' Days," even if Christmas fell on a Saturday or Sunday. Everyone, regardless of health, was expected to give a day of labor to society without pay. Remarkably, we began to look upon these days as festive occasions and even looked forward to them. At Easter, people brought delicious cakes and exquisitely colored eggs. After we had done light jobs such as tidying up the workplace, we had dinner and drank vodka. The mood was jolly. Although the government did not encourage religion, and few people went to church to worship or pray, the time-honored Christmas and Easter traditions remained with us. Even the Communist leaders slyly celebrated these holidays with their families. In our family, my grandmother always prepared for Easter by cleaning the house, baking cakes and coloring eggs. All the family, including Father, helped her. Father was not religious, but he enjoyed celebrating Easter and Christmas by singing the old folk songs and Christmas carols accompanied by music from our guitar and piano. Most importantly, we were all having fun together.

I was twenty in 1968, when I married Alexander Serebrovsky. He had been born and raised in Baku, the oil center in the Caucasus. Now Father's regard for Stalin came under assault from an unexpected quarter. My husband had personal reasons for hating Stalin, and I had brought him right into the bosom of the family. I have not forgotten our New Year's dinner in 1972. It was to be a grand family occasion, and we arrived at Father's home in a festive mood for the traditional feast. Unfortunately, the discussion during dinner turned to politics. It began when Alexander innocently mentioned that Stalin was guilty of crimes before, during, and after the war. Father replied that it was not Stalin who killed innocent people, but the secret police. In his response, Alexander did not reveal what had happened to his relative for whom he had been named. Rather, he told of his sister Nadia, who, when she was sixteen, spent a month in 1951 visiting the Gulaj-Pole region in western Ukraine. There she had heard many stories of the people's cruel suffering in the famine of 1931-33, and that Stalin was to blame. When she returned to Baku, she told these shocking stories to Alexander, who was thirteen. Father retorted that these were just hearsay and had nothing to do with "real history." Alexander countered by reminding Father that Khrushchev accused Stalin for the imprisonment and death of thousands, or even millions, of innocent Soviet citizens. Father replied heatedly that it was Beria, not Stalin, who was guilty of these crimes.[49] Beria, he said, did these heinous things without Stalin's knowledge.

What began as a discussion, now became an argument. With sharpness in his voice, Alexander reminded father that Khrushchev himself had said that it was impossible for these things to have occurred without Stalin's approval, and that Beria had acted upon Stalin's orders. Articles directly implicating Stalin had appeared in the press. Alexander went on to say that, to learn the truth, Father needed only talk to those whose relatives and friends had been arrested by the secret police and then disappeared.

Father was agitated. "Stalin wouldn't do that to his own people!" he cried.

"Stalin was paranoid," Alexander exclaimed. "He would do anything if he had even the least suspicion his power was being threatened!"

Far from impressing Father, Alexander's arguments only made him angry. Father now accused Alexander of being cynical and unpatriotic. As the argument got out of control, the talk became even more heated. Mother and I sat helplessly by as these two locked horns; a young male was challenging the dominant bull.

Finally, Father shouted at Alexander: "You have no right to slander Stalin and the Soviet Union! You did nothing to defend our

---

49 Lavrenty Pavlovich Beria (1899-1953), the Deputy Prime Minister for security within the Soviet Union from 1941 to 1953, was possibly the most hated and feared man in the Soviet Union.

Motherland! I did! I and my brothers-in-arms fought to the death! We were the ones who defeated the Nazis! We went into battle with the words on our lips, 'For the Motherland! For Stalin!'"

Wounded by this outburst, Alexander angrily stood up from the table, his meal unfinished. Taking me and our young daughter with him, he left Father's apartment and went home. Over the next few days, Alexander's anger was replaced by sadness. During our courtship and the four years of our marriage thus far, Alexander, now 34, had had the greatest respect for Father. But he was perplexed and disappointed that Father, with his wisdom and half a century of experience, did not see the evidence all around him.

For Father, the first direct challenge to his long-held beliefs had come from within his own family. He regretted his anger, but did not apologize. Harsh words have a price. For months, our family relationships remained cordial on the surface, but were strained, as happens when some subject must be avoided. In the following year, 1973, our second daughter, Nadia, was born. Father now had two granddaughters, and he could hardly afford to let politics interfere with the more precious vocation of grandfather. He began to treat Alexander with greater deference. He sought Alexander's opinion on non-political topics. He took Alexander fishing, perhaps the highest compliment Father could pay. Slowly, the breach healed.

א

As trust between the two men grew, Alexander unfolded how Stalin's purges had affected his own family's "real history." At first Alexander only told of a man in Baku, Alexander Pavlovich Serebrovsky, who had a name similar to his own. Later, when he felt Father was ready, Alexander revealed that Serebrovsky was his grandfather's cousin. After what happened to Serebrovsky, fear of the consequences had forced Alexander and his family to deny a blood relationship during, and even after, the dangerous Stalin years. Alexander learned the details of Serebrovsky's life from his mother, his aunt, and from avid reading of accounts of his famous relative in the Baku newspapers and in Soviet books.[50]

Serebrovsky, the idealistic son of a teacher, had enthusiastically embraced the concepts of Communism. In 1903, at the age of nineteen, he joined the Party and became friends with Lenin. Several times, Serebrovsky was arrested by Czarist agents, and each time he managed to escape. In 1908, following one of his legendary escapes from the agents, he met Lenin in Paris. Lenin encouraged him to study abroad, which he did for three years in Brussels and obtained a technical degree. By 1912, he was back in Russia. In the October Revolution of 1917, he led a company of Bolsheviks in the assault on the Winter Palace in St. Petersburg. After the revolution, Soviet economy was moribund. To resurrect the petroleum industry in the Caucasus, Lenin appointed Serebrovsky Chairman of the Baku Oil Committee on April 16, 1920.

Serebrovsky's first act was to open the rail line for transport of oil products to the Russian Soviet. The bridge that crossed the Kura river west of Baku had been damaged in the Civil War, and French engineers said that repairs would take months. Serebrovsky decided otherwise. He ordered supports to be built from huge wooden boxes, which were then filled with stones and cement. He rotated the work crews—ten minutes in the icy waters were followed by thirty minutes to rewarm on the bank. Within three days the supports were in place, and on the fourth day, with Serebrovsky standing triumphantly underneath, a train passed over the bridge. By 1 May, oil was flowing to Russia and respect was flowing to Serebrovsky.

One year later, in April 1921, Lenin wrote to him: "We are very poor. You must help us to buy all necessary industrial equipment, food, and clothing in exchange for oil and oil products." In May, the freighter *Georgia*, loaded with petroleum products bound for Europe and with Serebrovsky on board, became the first ship to

50 Alexander Pavlovich Serebrovsky is mentioned in Havin (1968) and Levytsky (1974).

fly the flag of the Union of Soviet Socialist Republics through the Straits of Bosporus.

From 1913 to 1927, Serebrovsky increased Baku gasoline production fifteenfold. He modernized the primitive Soviet gold industry and increased production fourfold. He also distinguished himself in the production of other non-ferrous metals and in the coal mining industry. He was a member of the Soviet Party Congress and was awarded the Order of the Soviet Union. His motto for the Party was: "More trust in each other, more mutual understanding, more cooperation in work." Despite this impressive record, Serebrovsky's three visits to the United States had aroused Stalin's suspicions that he had come under foreign influences.

In 1937, Serebrovsky was arrested and convicted of being "an enemy of the people." He was subsequently executed. His wife, Elena, disappeared into the concentration camp in Karaganda, which had been set up "for wives of the nation's enemies." Ironically, those who really believed that Communism could improve the life of ordinary citizens were often the very ones whom Stalin chose to eliminate. Many captains of Soviet industry were eliminated by Stalin during his years of the Great Terror.

Immediately after Serebrovsky's arrest, my husband's father, Nikolai Serebrovsky, was summoned for interrogation by the secret police. Apparently, they wanted to establish his connection to Alexander Pavlovich Serebrovsky to show that the two of them had worked together. Nikolai always denied any relationship and answered that he did not know Alexander Pavlovich at all; they simply shared the same last name. This denial was necessary to protect himself and his family. Over the next few months, the police repeatedly summoned and interrogated my husband's father and mother. Alexander's mother told her young son what was happening but, for his own safety, warned him not to speak of it outside the family. Alexander had come to believe that Stalin was the instigator of the purges of the innocent and the deaths of his relatives. This, together with the threat to himself and his own family, caused Alexander to accept Khrushchev's denunciations of Stalin in the Twentieth Party Congress.[51]

After that Congress, a memorial brass plate was installed with the inscription: "In this house lived Alexander Pavlovich Serebrovsky, the founder of Azerbaijan Oil Corporation." My husband never knew his famous relative, but he did often visit the house because his aunt, Asya Belenkaya, still lived there. In the house was a library containing more than eight thousand volumes, about half of them written in the several foreign languages that Alexander Pavlovich and Elena read and spoke fluently. As this story unfolded, it made a great impression on Father.

א

From 1975 onwards, Alexander and I, with our three young children, Zoya, Nadia, and Sergey, rented a country house each summer in the village of Glebovka on the Teterev River, fifteen miles upstream from its junction with the Dnieper. A migration from Kiev to the Teterev became our annual summer custom. By now, the family had become amicable again, and Father and Mother often visited us there, as did Father's younger sister from L'viv, Nina Drugova, and her husband. Father was a most inveterate mushroomer, and had a love for mushrooms second only to fishing. In an almost daily ceremony, we went on hikes to hunt for mushrooms. We knew every path and clearing by heart, and which mushrooms would be found in each. Sometimes, early in the morning, we would hunt for very special mushrooms, such as chanterelles or rissoles, or saffron. Every day, no matter what the weather, Father awoke before dawn and followed the river deep into the forest to fish. He also found time to teach his grandchildren how to find their way through the forest without getting lost, and how to make a fire in the rain.

51 Khrushchev's entire speech to the Twentieth Party Congress on 25 February 1956 is given in Khrushchev Remembers as Appendix 4 (1970).

Alexander built us two kayaks with which we explored the river. Also during these summers, he taught each of our children to swim using his own original method. First of all, on the riverbank, he held long discussions with them on the theory of swimming. Next, in a basin of water, they practiced putting their faces under the surface. Then there were swimming exercises on the sand. Finally, when he felt that the preparation was complete, he fastened a rope around the child under the arms and, maintaining control of the rope from the boat, threw him or her into the river. Each child learned to swim within two days! When the children were older, we began to take long kayak camping trips along the rivers of this region, and especially along the Teterev. For our whole family, these summers were a retreat into nature for the restoration of our souls.

In 1985, Father, now sixty-three, reduced his work schedule to part-time hours. In superb health and with boundless energy, he now began to look for other things to do. It was at this time that he decided to write his memoirs, and the research for them required much of his attention.

In addition, his interest in fishing grew. In previous years, he had already found the loveliest parts of the Teterev River. During his high-school years in Zhitomyr, Father had lived in a house beside this river. It was there that he had begun to fish, and it was along this river that he had courted Mother. Stretches of the Teterev are nature's own paradise, where the riverbanks are covered with huge, towering pines. In its streams are great quantities of fish, and on its forested banks are game birds of every description, including, of course, the grouse for which it is named.

To the Teterev came the Czars and, more recently, the Communist bosses, Khrushchev, Brezhnev, Sherbitsky and Shelest, to hunt from huts constructed for just that purpose. Deer, wild boar, pheasants, and peacocks were raised on special farms and then released into the area to await their fate from the guns of these dignitaries. To fish, our leaders floated along the streams in beautiful little houses built on pontoons. Of course, all of these areas were guarded. Why, Father wondered, should this beautiful area be restricted to the

Party bosses if, according to Party doctrine, it belonged to all the people? He had found secret passages and covert paths into some of the more secluded and unguarded parts of this sacred preserve. He loved to fish there and to bring his family. Having our whole family together, seeing our children grow up swimming like fishes and learning to love the outdoors—these were happy years.

During the thirty-two years from Stalin's death until Father's partial retirement in 1985, the mood of our country changed. As Stalin's purges and the Great Patriotic War receded into the past, the whole population experienced a gradual change in sentiment, which became apparent in the celebration of our holidays. One example was the holiday on 1 May, which had caused me so much trouble in 1956. By the late 1970s, public enthusiasm for Communist celebrations had already waned. It even became necessary for the chiefs to order people to participate in the parade or risk losing their jobs. The changing leadership contributed to our changing mood. After Stalin, we had Khrushchev, and then, in 1964, Brezhnev. Following the death of Brezhnev in 1982, there was a rapid succession of leaders—Andropov in 1982, Chernenko in 1984, and then, in March of 1985, Mikhail Gorbachev. Soon after Gorbachev came to power, he loosened media censorship, and Stalin's atrocities were the subject of much discussion on radio, television, and in the newspapers. People talked more and more openly about the purges of their families and friends. None of these changes were lost on Father.

Our family, as well as our country, had experienced change; our lives had improved. During this period, we need not fight an invading enemy. We were no longer hungry. Typhus, tuberculosis, and cholera did not threaten us. Motorized transport, air travel, and television became necessities for us. Our family members were well educated. We accepted the cultural advantages of literature, music, drama, and history. Father had leisure time and a comfortable income. We had the luxury of vacations in pristine natural settings. Two generations earlier, with the First World War, the Civil War, the Purges and famines, and the Great Patriotic War, my grandparents could say none of these things. These advantages we now enjoyed were also enjoyed by millions of others in the Soviet Union. It was ironic that a cultured, educated middle class—a kind of bourgeoisie—had arisen within Communism's ostensibly classless society. Independently-thinking men and women had received the intellectual and emotional tools that permitted them to question the Communist practices of previous generations. Not only my husband Alexander, but many other intellectuals began to question the motives of Soviet leaders. These fundamental changes allowed the people of the Soviet Union to challenge the country's involvement in a war in Afghanistan—a war whose initial phases were observed by Father's younger brother, Gregory. Father was also not immune to the societal changes. He ceased to speak of Stalin with respect; those feelings had been overtaken and overwhelmed by an inevitable march of events. He still clung to the Party, but he was beginning to awaken.

Tatiana V. Kramchaninova-Serebrovska

15

The Soviet Tragedy of Afghanistan

Gregory Kramchaninov, Viktor's younger brother

All brutalized by fate,
Fierce fighting every night takes place,
With murder, violence and hate,
Their judgments short and merciless.

From *Princess Troubetzkoy* by Nikolai Nekrasov (1821-1878)[52]

א

In 1948, I entered the L'viv Polytechnical Institute. Though my studies were hard, my life immediately became better, because the government provided for my education, lodging, and clothing—and I got enough to eat! I loved to sing, and I joined the Institute's chorus. There I met a young woman, Ludmila Fedotova. We had both been in the high-school chorus in Zhitomyr, and she had come to L'viv to study cardiology at the Medical Institute. Although I didn't remember her, she remembered me. In L'viv, we now became friends, then more than friends, and we married in 1951. Viktor and Maria came from Kiev to L'viv for the wedding. They brought with them their four-year-old daughter, Tatiana, who stole the show. After the ceremony, we all sang our patriotic song "We are all for peace, the people swear." Tatiana sat high on Vik-

52 Published in English translation by Soskice (1977, p22).

tor's shoulders. She sang loudly and remarkably well for a child of four, but she made up her own words.

After our marriage, I spent two more years at the Institute, and they were perhaps the happiest of my life. We say that when you are with your darling, even a hut can be paradise. Everything seemed to get better, and petroleum engineering itself took on a rosy glow. My marriage to Ludmila had yet another benefit for which I have always been grateful: when we were in Afghanistan, her presence may have saved my life.

After graduating in 1953 and having done well academically, I was sent by the government on several important assignments. Ludmila and I went first to the Russian city of Kazan where, ten years before, Viktor had awaited his new bomber to roll out of the factory. I was then sent to the Caucasus—Georgia, Azerbaijan, and Armenia—where I directed construction of the Trans-Caucasian gas pipeline. I also helped build an arterial pipeline supplying gas to the Soviet Union from Iran.

Then came my unpleasant time in Afghanistan. I was no stranger to adversity; from age thirteen to fifteen, I had lived through the Nazi occupation of Zhitomyr. In those years, my youth was an advantage. Teenagers don't think much about danger, and there was comfort in being with my father and elder brother. They made me skillful in avoiding enemy soldiers. Foraging through Nazi camps, stealing their food, siphoning gasoline from their vehicles, hiding from their troops in a leaf-covered ditch, and listening to forbidden radio broadcasts were all dangerous, but exciting. While youth can turn adversity into adventure, at age fifty, danger is only danger. Some have said that life as a Soviet advisor in Afghanistan after 1979 was a happy and even luxurious existence. That was not my experience. During my two years in Afghanistan, the work was hard, understanding the culture and language was impossible, and danger was always present.

Of Afghan history, I knew little more than that Mohammed Daoud had conducted a palace *coup* against the king, Mohammed Shah, in 1973 and had declared the country a republic and himself the president. The sending of Soviet civilians to Afghanistan was precipitated by the military *coup d'etat* of 27 April 1978. A group of Afghan officers, called the People's Democratic Party of Afghanistan, had set up a government modeled after the Central Asian Socialist Republics. The leader, Nur Mohammed Taraki, pressed hard for progressive change in Afghanistan and appealed to the Soviet Union for economic and military aid. The United States of America opposed this expansion of socialism, and encouraged the upper bourgeoisie, rich merchants, businessmen, and some high-ranking military officers to rebel against Taraki's government.[53] In order to "stabilize our southern border," our government responded with what it called "disinterested help": equipment, machinery, and material.

Our government also began sending thousands of its own citizens as advisors. Some were military, some were experienced in Soviet politics and government, and some were civilian specialists in technical, economic, or legal fields. The technical specialists, like myself, were to build bridges, dams, houses, hospitals, schools, and other installations. I was to build automated military gasoline storage depots to service automobiles, airplanes, armored cars, and tanks, and to do it I would supervise a group of Afghan riggers and workers. Every military unit had civilian specialists and advisors; I was one of these and was assigned to the General Staff of the Soviet Army, Special Detachment #10. My detachment had other civilian specialists to supervise many kinds of construction. In addition to all this, the Soviet Union was helping Afghanistan improve its military forces by providing defense technology, armaments, and military advisers, and by training Afghan military and civilian specialists in the Soviet Union. It was a massive effort.

Fortunately, Ludmila volunteered to go with me, even though we had to leave our thirteen-year-old daughter Elena with my sister, Nina Drugova, in L'viv. Ludmila and I, with other civilian specialists

53 As early as 1973, the United States established a training center in Pakistan for "potential Afghan guerillas" (Sarin and Dvoretsky, 1993).

and their wives, went to Moscow for official processing. On March 7, 1979, we obtained approval and all the appropriate documents. I remember well the next day, for it was unusually spring-like—bright and sunny—and the Muscovites were hurriedly purchasing flowers to congratulate the ladies on our esteemed International Women's Day. Then, innocent of difficulties, we flew to an unknown land under the roar of aircraft engines—a far more peaceful sound than we were soon destined to hear.

We were unprepared for turmoil, but we were soon to see it for ourselves. After landing at the capital city of Kabul, we busily settled into the quarters for Soviet specialists and advisors—five-story buildings right in the heart of the city. That night, we had barely unpacked when we heard bursts of machine-gun fire and shell explosions coming from different directions. Artillery cannonades from the distant mountains reached our ears. Nighttime battles were being fought. A few days after our arrival, the western Afghan city of Herat erupted in open revolt. Soviet specialists and their families were murdered and their bodies dragged through the streets. The Afghan troops sent to restore order defected, and escalating violence ensued. Suddenly we realized that Afghanistan was far from peaceful.

Kabul was relatively calm. On the streets, we easily identified Soviet citizens as Russian speaking non-Afghans in western dress. Although we were a large civilian presence, Soviet soldiers were seldom seen. Many Afghans in Kabul seemed satisfied with the Soviet-style government; they had a better standard of living, their children began to go to school, and their healthcare improved. However, the security in the rest of Afghanistan was in the unsteady hands of the Afghan Army. Peasants in the countryside rioted against the government, which they believed to be anti-Muslim and Soviet-dominated. Government troops were unreliable. It was civil war.

It seemed to me that religion was a root cause of the fighting. Religion is all-pervasive in Afghanistan. Fundamentalist mullahs teach that Allah is a god who barely tolerates non-Muslims, and that even believers are punished when they deviate from religious law. Their religion is political, seeking a purely Islamic government, where revenge and violence are acceptable to achieve political ends. These mullahs opposed the removal of the *burkha*, the garment that traditionally covered Afghan women from head to toe. They opposed free education for all children. They opposed women having rights equal to men. They stirred up the peasants, declaring that the government's policies were against Islamic culture. In many places across the land, peasants formed bandit groups, which were supported by money, weapons, and even combatants from Muslim countries such as Iran, Pakistan, and Saudi Arabia.

Tribal differences were another cause of unrest. While nearly all Afghans are Muslim—either Shiite or Sunni—there are different tribes, which are often at war with each other. The numerous Pashtun tribe, who are largely Shiite, live near the borders with Pakistan and China. The Sunni live near Iran. In the north are the Tajik. Whoever enjoys the support of the Pashtun tribe commands the most power in the country, and, unfortunately, the Council of Pashtun had agreed to oppose the People's Democratic Party, which they saw as a Soviet instrument. That had spelled trouble. With the Muslims fighting among themselves as well as against the government in Kabul, there was plenty of violence in the country. We had been thrown into a boiling political cauldron—a country seething with unrest—and had not been warned.

The political situation deteriorated further. In September, six months after we arrived, Hafizullah Amin, who had been an assistant to Taraki, accomplished a military *coup*.[54] Taraki's government fell, and with it the People's Democratic Party. As insurance against retaliation, Amin executed Taraki, his family, and his political allies. Amin belonged to a pro-American political circle and hoped to receive support from the United States. However, Amin had made his bed, and now he had to lie in it. Our Politburo saw Amin as hostile and dangerous to our interests. To "stabilize our southern border,"

54 Taraki's secret police had failed twice to assassinate Amin, who retaliated by promoting a military *coup*, which deposed Taraki (Anwar, 1988).

our army invaded Afghanistan in December of 1979. When it occupied the Presidential Palace in Kabul, Amin died in the fighting. Bobrak Karmal, a comrade-in-arms of Taraki, became president of the country. Military occupation of Afghanistan and a most tragic period for the Soviet Union began.

Only in cities where government troops were stationed was there relative calm. But even there, on some nights, our soldiers skirmished with invisible adversaries. Our military suffered casualties, as did the peaceful inhabitants. Our tanks stood on the main streets and at strategic points. Patrols checked documents, and anyone without them could be shot. In all Afghan cities, a curfew was imposed from 8 AM until 6 PM. In the countryside between cities, the roads were controlled by our enemies, whom we called "dushmen," from the Persian word *dush*, meaning "bad." Dushmen controlled sixty percent of the mountainous terrain, and they behaved with impunity. Because of them, we had to travel from one city to another by airplane or helicopter. Even in the cities, we moved between office and home in special enclosed cars. Every day we were told that all was well, yet we were warned not to venture far from our compound. The officials seemed not to notice this contradiction.

Of course, all was not well. During the day in the countryside, dushmen were peasants working the land, or they were combatants hiding in slit trenches, camouflaged from aerial reconnaissance. But at night, they became militaristic. As soon as darkness fell, dushmen emerged and began to fire on our construction sites, apartments, and airdromes. Our forces returned the fire. Somehow we got used to sleeping through the small arms fire, the artillery barrages, and the shell bursts. The skirmishes ceased in the daytime only to begin again at night. We civilian specialists had no personal guard; we were on our own. We were armed for self-defense at all times.

Military action or not, I had a job to do—namely, to construct two petroleum storage depots in Kabul, one in Jalalabad, one in Khost, and one in Kandahar. At any development site, we had five or six Soviet engineers representing different specialties, and each of us had about twenty-five Afghan workers in his crew. We engineers were working at more than one site simultaneously, and in my case, I needed to assemble six crews of Afghan men. Some were laborers, and some, who had worked abroad in Pakistan or Iran, had skills in carpentry, plumbing, or electrical work. Except for ceasing work to pray three times a day, the Afghans were good workers, and put in their eight-hour days without complaint. They were desperately poor, and no matter what they thought of us Soviet civilians, they were glad to have a job, so that they could feed themselves and their families. They had almost no education, but every ten days, each man was able to sign for his paycheck.

I never knew how much the Afghans were paid. The money went directly from Moscow to Kabul, so our workers' salaries came from their own government. Without oil a machine will not run, so the Afghan workers must have been paid enough. On paydays, I opened a bottle of vodka and celebrated with the Afghan foremen of our construction crews. Despite the Muslim prohibitions against alcohol, these foremen drank with pleasure, but I never knew if they drank alcohol when they were just among themselves. They were not shy, but when we got together, informal communication was difficult. I understood little of the Dari tongue, the Afghan variant of Persian, and they did not speak Russian. If I asked a question about their families, the answer came with only a word or two and a lot of gestures. They never asked me about life in the Soviet Union, and I never spoke to them about religion or politics.

An issue always in the back of my mind was that of trust. In the Soviet Union, I had developed over the years an effective style for solving either technical or personnel problems on the job: I simply had a conference with my workers over a bottle of vodka. By the time the bottle was empty, the problem had usually been solved, friendships had been built, and trust established. In this way, I could build teams that worked well together. Because of the cultural and linguistic differences, this strategy wouldn't work in Afghanistan. I used a simpler strategy—namely, to treat my work crews with kindness. They seemed to respond, for they were socially cordial to me in return. I had no reason to believe that any of them were dushmen by night, but how could I be sure? Even if they were not dushmen themselves, they might have friends who were. How could intensely devout men who prayed several times a day trust me, an atheist? To the Muslim extremist, a nonbeliever is considered a low form of life. I could not distinguish a potentially violent religious zealot from a rational, moderate, peaceful Muslim, and the language barrier didn't help. My work crew seemed to trust each other. Perhaps they were from the same ethnic group or the same tribe; one raven never puts out the eye of its fellow. But I felt some tension between me and my Afghan crews. Were they uncomfortable with me because I was their boss, or because I was an infidel? One who has been taught from childhood that Allah controls everything might not trust the decisions of a non-believer.

When I stepped beyond engineering, I saw how little weight my opinion carried. It happened one day that one of my workers badly injured a finger. I attempted to stop the bleeding, and instructed him to lie down until I could get an ambulance to take him to the hospital. He responded by saying, "Allah is displeased with me!" and, taking an ax, he promptly chopped off his finger. My offer of help had not impressed him. Apparently, he was certain of Allah's judgment and that Allah would accept a severed finger as atonement for whatever sin he had committed. Dismemberment was highly prized among religious fundamentalists in Afghan society. Differences in our spoken languages were insignificant compared to differences in our cultures. How were we to understand each other? And, without understanding, how could I trust my work crews, and they me?

Uncertain of our safety and far from home, we looked to our own countrymen for companionship. Many of the Soviet advisors in our compound had brought their families with them, and we soon became a community of friends in these anxious times. In the battles against the dushmen, some of our advisors were wounded and others killed. We were all at risk, but the military advisors were particularly vulnerable, for their units were sometimes ambushed by Mujahadeen rebel bands. The friendships within our compound helped to comfort and support the wives during periods of agonizing suspense when their husbands were away on a mission. Ludmila remained alone when I was away on my frequent trips to other cities. It was a happy event for the whole community when a man returned home safely. Community support was even more important when a man did not return, and his body was sent back to the Soviet Union in a zinc coffin. Then, we rallied around the families of our lost friends and rendered whatever support we could.

Because Ludmila was a physician, she looked after the medical needs of the advisors and their families, and she also helped them with personal problems. Her reputation as a physician soon spread beyond our compound, and she began to see patients from Afghan families, particularly women and children, who were delighted to see a female physician. Women received almost no medical care, because most Afghan doctors were men, and there were cultural and religious prohibitions preventing them from examining women. Thus Ludmila provided health care where it had not been available before. Sometimes Ludmila also took care of Afghan men. One patient was an Afghan man with heart trouble. She may have also helped his wife or other members of his family. We do not remember exactly what help she gave, but favors done and not remembered are the most effective. At any rate, the man was grateful, and in Afghan society kindness is rewarded.

One day in June 1980, her Afghan patient advised her not to be at home that night, and we followed his advice. When we returned to our apartment the following morning, we found the bodies of two of our closest friends outside our front door. Their ears had been cut off and their eye sockets were empty. The dushmen had done this, transported the bodies, and then dumped them at our door. Had our friends been tortured prior to being murdered? What kind of culture was this? Ludmila and I could hardly believe what had happened. We and everyone in our compound were shocked that human beings could behave in such a way. We were all grief-stricken and angry.

I needed to express my sorrow and rage. That very night I sat and poured out my soul in a poem, which I sent back to my family. To get it past the censors, I wrote it on toilet paper and hid it inside a toilet paper roll. A friend carried it out of Afghanistan and sent the poem to Viktor. Writing it helped me to deal with the turmoil in my heart.

Gregory Kramchaninov, age seventy-four, showing the poem about Afghanistan that he had written on toilet paper in Kabul in 1980. A friend smuggled the poem past the censors and sent it to Viktor in Kiev.

AFGHANISTAN

Dedicated to my brother, Viktor, in memory of Afghanistan
—June 1980

Mountain peaks,
Groves and fields,
Sunny distances,
Desert ground,
Abrupt gorges,
Cold and heat,
Nomadic tribes,
Pashtun and Dari.
Three wives,
Ancient customs,
With prayers
Every day.
Clay huts,
No fruitful ground.
And from Islam
Animal spite.
We came from the North
To improve their life,
To secure our border.
It's important for us.
They want no help.
Eyes dark with wrath,
They stab our back,
A rite for foreigners.
America, beyond the sea,
And Pakistan, China nearby,
All play dirty with us
Every day.
While dollars flow
Like a river
Damned dushmen

Kill us.
Mothers anguish.
Families grieve.
Our young men perish,
All for nothing.
We thought them noble,
A proud people—but no.
All are corrupt,
"our true friends."
Such "true friendship"
Costs very much.
There is not enough zinc
For coffins.
They follow the mullah,
Like goats.
His word is law
This native brother.
He calls to kill
All infidels.
They follow
As goats in a storm.
To make from goats
A real people,
Will take
Many days.
But our cause is just.
We will prevail.
Even if they cut off our ears
And tear out our eyes.[55]

Our two murdered friends had been away from Kabul working in a distant city and, not having being warned as we had been, they had fallen victim to this atrocity. We do not know how many others

55 Gregory's poem has been translated literally and without regard for rhyme.

of our people were killed that night, and in so brutal a fashion, because censorship restricted our information, and the bodies were hastily shipped back to the Soviet Union. We lived in a tight-knit, closed community and did not see the greater picture. Gradually, we learned by word of mouth that the Pashtuns had planned a rampage for that evening in several cities. We also heard that leaders of the dushmen had paid large sums of money to their soldiers for tossing mutilated corpses into the residence compounds of our people. They wanted to undermine morale of the civilian specialists. Such sadism occurred rather frequently in Afghanistan, but these acts of intimidation failed; they only drew us closer together and increased our resolve.

After the initial shock had abated, Ludmila and I began to ask ourselves some unpleasant questions. Why were *we* chosen to have the bodies dumped outside *our* door? These bodies had been brought to our specific apartment; did the dushmen know these two men were our closest friends? Were the assassins disappointed that I was not at home? Did they have a similar fate in mind for me? For Ludmila too? What would have happened had Ludmila's patient not advised us to be away from home on this particular night? Did her Afghan patient warn her out of gratitude, or did he not want to lose her services as a physician? How did he know what would happen and when? Our questions were never answered. We became ever more vigilant. On the job, I began to observe the Afghans on my crew and on other crews more closely.

How could the Mujahadeen deliberately torture and kill innocent people? It seemed to me that such behavior arose from an inherent violence developed since childhood. These were illiterate men whose religion permeated everything: their culture, laws, courts, treatment of women and children, family life, and customs. Theirs was a ritualistic religion, where prayers were at fixed times of the day and were aimed at an established destination. During the prayers, everyone moved together like sheep in a herd with prescribed body positions. The men accepted what the mullahs told them about the Koran, about what they should believe and how they should behave.

Expressing doubt was out of the question. Clearly, radical mullahs taught their followers vengeance and violence without mentioning Islam's redeeming features of kindness and mercy.

In 1981, I was recalled to the Soviet Union. With relief, we left a country of contradictions. Educated, barefaced women in Kabul contrasted with illiterate, *burkha*-covered women in the countryside. Men working side-by-side with us to build a better life were opposed by others working against us to destroy what we had built. Students studying in the university welcomed the Soviet-style change, but rural peasants opposed education. Some mullahs advised progress and restraint, while others taught revenge and retribution. Strong family ties existed, as did strong antagonisms between clans. Clans agreeing to oppose the Afghan government fought among themselves. The country had rich natural resources, but the people were poor. How can a nation prosper when many of its people despise education, and when women are virtually slaves? When we left Afghanistan, our lives became easier, but there was no respite for our friends who remained, nor for our country.

After my return to Kiev, I spent many evenings over food and vodka with Viktor, discussing the war in Afghanistan. Having been with the partisans in 1943, he knew how the dushmen could ambush our military columns. Viktor saw how religious fanaticism was rife among the Afghan population. He understood my poem and the cruelty I had witnessed. But the questions remained: Why did we go into Afghanistan? Was it just to "stabilize our southern border"?

Now that two decades have passed, I have come to think that the idea of Soviet expansion still warmed the hearts of our leaders. Our Politburo had suffered defeat in 1973, when the murder of President Allende[56] in Chile ended the socialist government there, and our leaders had been criticized for being too inactive. Then in 1979, when President Amin of Afghanistan requested American support,

56 Salvador Allende Gossens (1908-1973) was socialist president of Chile from 1970 until he was killed in a military *coup* in 1973 led by General Augusto Pinochet.

they felt called upon to answer a direct threat to Soviet borders. In addition, they saw Afghanistan, with its poor, uneducated, and discordant population, as easy prey. The decision to invade was not Chairman Brezhnev's alone—he was too weak-headed—but was a collective decision of the Politburo, goaded by the Minister of Defense. Our leaders' mania for expansion drove us into Afghanistan.

But for what? To impose our culture and philosophy on such a people by military means was impossible. Whatever we built up would surely be torn down. The risks were too great—not only for soldiers, but also for civilians. The Afghan war lasted until 1989— a period of almost ten years. More than 13,000 Soviet soldiers were killed and 70,000 wounded. Many of the wounded became invalids. How many women were widowed? How many mothers had to bring up children with no father?

I returned from Afghanistan at the age of fifty-three and retired at sixty-five. Now, at seventy-three, I am confined to my house with Parkinson's disease, but two life experiences remain indelibly etched on my memory—the Nazi occupation of Zhitomyr, and the loss of my friends in Afghanistan.

As I write these words with a shaking hand, never to be steady again, Afghanistan is once more on the world's stage. Americans now write the script and perform the drama. The question is: can their politicians preserve the innocent, promote the common welfare, and insure the peace? In our case, the Afghan war was the result of the mindless policies of our politicians. It tore our country apart, demoralized our society, and contributed greatly to the break-up of the Soviet Union. In the end, the Afghans were not better off. What will happen this time? Will America and Afghanistan fare better?

Gregory Kramchaninov

16

Chernobyl: Viktor's Moment of Truth

Tatiana Kramchaninova-Serebrovska

How pitiless are men!
To hide the truth - why was there need?
From *Princess Troubetzkoy* by Nikolai Nekrasov (1821-1878)[57]

א

The Chernobyl nuclear disaster occurred in 1986. That spring, Alexander and I planned a family boating vacation. We worked weekends over the winter and accumulated enough time to extend the traditional May Day holiday by two weeks. With the decreasing popularity of Communist celebrations, we no longer risked our jobs by failing to appear in the May Day parade. It was now mostly for children anyway, and attendance was not required even for them, so we could skip the parade and go boating instead. Zoya was just finishing high school. Nadia was now thirteen, Sergey twelve. We five, along with our gear and food, fit nicely into the two kayaks Alexander had built. During the last week of April and the first week of May, spring would be beginning, the trees would be blooming, and paddling along would be lovely. We chose our favorite river for the trip, the beautiful Teterev, unconcerned that, as it emptied into the Dnieper, it was in the shadow of the Chernobyl nuclear power station.

57 Published in English translation by Soskice (1977, p30).

On April 24, we put in our boats and began paddling down the river through an unspoiled, deserted region. Saturday, April 26 was very windy. We could not understand why all of us felt so listless. Even Alexander, whose robust energy was legendary, was not up to par. After we had paddled for only a short distance, he declared that we should set up camp early, so we pitched our tent on the riverbank. We could not have known that earlier that morning a reactor at Chernobyl had exploded, sending tons of radioactive material thousands of feet into the sky. We had no radio with us, but a radio would not have warned us, because the government made no public announcement. The next day, we continued our boat trip, coming closer and closer to Chernobyl. On April 30, we were startled by people shouting at us from the riverbank. With great excitement, they told us that something had happened downstream, and whatever it was had caused the police to cordon off the river. We did not believe them and continued down the river. There was no blockade; everything was peaceful. We thought they must have been misinformed or were playing some kind of joke. On May 2, we came upon some campers who had a radio and were listening to *Voice of America*. We now heard the reports with our own ears: an explosion and fire one week earlier had caused a massive release of radioactivity from the Chernobyl power plant, only a few miles from where we were!

We had to return home quickly. Being in the wilderness, getting back was not easy. Each kayak weighed a hundred and ten pounds, and we had five rucksacks weighing forty pounds each. We struggled with this mass for six miles through the forests until we came to a road where we could catch a bus to Kiev. Back in the city, confusion, shock, and despondency greeted us. On April 28, an official announcement to the rest of the world—not to the Soviet population—had stated only that "...one of the atomic reactors was damaged" at the Chernobyl power plant. Foreign radio stations, like *Voice of America* or *Liberty Life*, were broadcasting stories of a massive nuclear accident at Chernobyl. They reported that radioactivity from Chernobyl was being detected in nearly every country in Europe, having drifted hundreds or thousands of miles. These stories spreading through the population caused great alarm, because Chernobyl was our neighbor, being only ninety miles to the north. The May Day parade had taken place as usual with thousands of children and youth marching in the streets. "Surely," people said, "our government would have called off the parade rather than expose our children to dangerous radioactivity." People just did not know what to believe, and our government told us nothing.

On May 2, our government made a short vague statement, which only increased the rumors. Finally, on May 3 came an official announcement of a nuclear disaster at Chernobyl. Panic enveloped Kiev. Hundreds of thousands of hysterical people rushed to the railway station to send their children as far from Kiev as possible. For the next two days and nights, Alexander and I took turns standing in the queue to buy rail tickets to L'viv for our son, Sergey, and daughter, Nadia. Father managed to procure three airplane tickets, so that Mother and my sister Lena's two children could fly to Leningrad, where Mother had relatives. Within three days after the official announcement, Kiev was emptied of its children. Their laughter was not heard, and children were not seen in the streets.

Those who remained behind did not know what to expect or how to behave. What was safe to eat and drink? Television told us to stay indoors, close all windows, and wash what was worn outside each day. We were warned that the fallout contained radioactive iodine, even a little of which was harmful to the thyroid gland. We were told that we could protect ourselves by taking iodine that was not radioactive. People drank tincture of iodine mixed with milk without any idea of the proper dosage. As hysteria abated, depression followed. Alcohol consumption rose alarmingly. Many believed they were living their final days and sought whatever happiness and pleasure they could find. The mood in Kiev recalled the feasts during the plagues of the Middle Ages, when orgies occurred among those who felt they were facing certain death. But there was no increasing death, and over the next few days we began to adapt to the situation and even to joke about it. Eventually, the children and a more normal life returned.

Our eldest daughter, Zoya, remained in Kiev to take her final school examinations. Two years later, she married and became pregnant. For years, my fondest dream had been to have a grandchild. But her child was stillborn. I still believe that the radiation she received while we were so near to Chernobyl damaged her ovaries and her ability to carry the child. The reactor burned for ten days, continuing to send huge amounts of radioactivity into the air. The heaviest fallout was in the first days, while we were boating and innocent of the radioactive "rain." Being out in the open on the Teterev River, fully exposed to the sky, Zoya must have absorbed a high dose of radiation. Even so, I feel guilty for not evacuating her from Kiev. Why did I rely on the official information that, because she was older, Zoya did not need to be evacuated? By staying, she just got more radiation. Her baby died because of the radiation she received prior to her pregnancy. No one can convince me otherwise. I have continued to hope that my children would have children, but that has not happened. Chernobyl robbed me of my only grandchild!

While we were boating, Father, working at Kiev's main airdrome, was puzzled. From April 26, a great many children boarded airplanes, which then took off from side runways. He did not understand why the children were leaving Kiev early in the spring. They didn't usually leave the city until the schools were closed in summer, when they left to go to camp, to the Crimea for vacation, or to special sanatoria for rest and recreation. But school was not yet out. As the scene was repeated each day, his wonderment grew. Who were these children? With some detective work, Father learned they were from families of government officials. But why were they leaving Kiev? On May 3, when the government acknowledged the Chernobyl accident, Father understood. High-up government officials were secretly evacuating their own children by air.

Now Father also understood why the public announcement of the Chernobyl accident had been delayed for seven days. Officials had refused to make the announcement until their own children were safe. They knew that tons of radioactive material were being spewed into the sky each day not far to the north. They had deliberately put the thousands of Kiev children who were exposed for hours in the May Day parade at risk. The officials knew that prompt disclosure would have prompted us, the ordinary citizens, to protect our own children during these dangerous days, and that public panic would have interfered with getting their own children to safety. Now, for the first time, Father saw it clearly with his own eyes: when there was a choice between protecting the people or protecting their own families, the officials protected their own. Father saw the government unmasked. It stood naked before him; "the emperor had no clothes." *The Soviet government did not care for its people.* He exploded with anger. It was Father's moment of truth.

If it violates one's fundamental beliefs, a moment of truth is not easy. In Father's case, it violated teachings from his earliest childhood. Father's own parents, Panteley and Barbara, were poor and had eagerly grasped the socialist ideals that, with equality and brotherhood, everyone could work together to produce a happy, prosperous society. Father had learned well from his parents; the apple falls close to the tree. He learned not only from his parents, for in kindergartens, schools, pioneer camps, and elsewhere, the religion of Communism was substituted for God. For decades, Father said he had believed a monstrous lie as a child believes in a fairy story: "Communism will bring a radiant future, if only everyone will believe and do everything in their power to bring it about. One needs only to work, to wait, and to tolerate the hard times until it triumphs." Father had believed. Communism, he said, had promised everyone a sheepskin coat, but the promises were only warm words. The government had treated him like a condom, which it had used and then thrown away.

Father was not the only one who felt this way. After Chernobyl, people everywhere became disillusioned. They saw the hypocrisy of their government. They saw a Party leadership that had nothing in common with ordinary citizens. They saw a Party not under popular control. In the past, when the government had meted out cruel punishment or prison for little or no crime and had said it was for the common good, the people had been passive. Even this refinement of cruelty had been accepted. Now, however, people began to identify Communists with the secret police. Father had been regarded as a war hero, and he had basked in this glory, but now he ceased to be a hero due to his Communist ties. Worse, he became something of a villain. Some young people even reviled him for his Party membership. Father had been popular with young people and he took this very hard. It forced him to begin thinking about the Party and the government in a new way.

Father had always said that there was more to fishing than catching fish. In the silence on the river, he could think, and now contemplation brought him peace and a plan of action. One June day in 1986, he brought home a string of fish and his plan. "If we cannot trust our government to protect us," he said, "then we should protect ourselves. We will get ourselves a 'spare airdrome' as a safe haven from another atomic disaster." One could almost hear Barbara speaking—"One lives not by prayers, but by deeds." Father, Mother, Alexander, and myself pooled our resources to buy a *dacha* away from Kiev. We found one in the Poltava region, about ninety miles to the east and a journey of four hours by train. There were two acres of land, an old stone house, and an orchard. The land was fertile and the area was in a "clean zone," meaning it had escaped radiation fallout from Chernobyl. The *dacha* was within convenient walking distance of a railroad station, which was crucial, because we had no car. For our whole family, it was a retreat from the noise and bustle of Kiev, and for Father it was a new outlet for his restless energy.

Over the next few years, Father's disillusionments following Chernobyl were reinforced by Gorbachev's open policy of *glasnost.* Radio, television, and newspapers publicized stories that had previously been suppressed. Previously forbidden books became available to the general population. People could talk more freely. In January 1990, Father's airdrome reduced its staff, and he became fully retired. Always a lover of literature, he now had more time to read. Solzhenitsyn's writings were being broadly discussed. Father obtained a copy of *A Day in the Life of Ivan Denisovich* and reread it with new eyes, but it was *Gulag Archipelago* that made the greatest impact. It had been published serially in the Soviet magazine *Novy Mir*. Father and Mother sat hours at a time, reading it aloud and pausing to discuss it. They talked especially about a statement to a prisoner by one of the characters, a guard who said, "Stalin does not give a damn about you!" Father saw that Stalin's suspicious personality and his need for absolute power had led to a ruthlessness in the whole society. Father realized that he had been deceived by decades of propaganda glorifying Stalin and by tight control of the media, which hid his crimes and had prevented the people from knowing the truth.

Through this book, Mother and Father relived their lives, seeing them in a new light. The famines, the arrests and deaths of Serebrovsky and his wife, the presence of political deputies in the military units, the confiscation of Father's diary, the assignment of Mother to a remote medical post without regard for her young child, the teaching of Pioneers to spy on their parents, the cover-up of the Chernobyl disaster—these and other mysteries became clearer. Father was profoundly disturbed by the realization that, from early in the Soviet regime, thousands of innocent Soviet citizens had been executed, and millions of others were starved or sent to slave labor camps. He was saddened by the sheer magnitude and duration of the Soviet barbarity against its own people. Father wondered why he failed so long to understand that the Party was not interested in him, but only in itself, when the clues had been there all along. Why, he asked, had he faced death so often during the war with the words, "For Stalin!" He had been, he said, like a Ukrainian peasant who will not make the sign of the cross until the thunder bursts his eardrum.

But was it all in vain, the ideals to which he had clung, all his hopes and dreams, and all the goals toward which he had worked? Mother and Father debated this question. Father had read Orwell's *Animal Farm*, the parable on Communism and human nature. Society always contains greedy pigs ready to take advantage of the hard work of others. Because all people are flawed, Father questioned whether human beings could ever make Communism work. Still, though Communism had gone wrong, the idea that people should work together and care for each other was right. Bad people had taken a good idea and had ruined it for a country ready to believe in it. The Party, Father said, had used the idea of Communism as a general hypnosis for the people and had substituted it for religion. It was a remarkable phenomenon that social scientists must someday explore.

Many others felt that Communism had gone awry. Like soap bubbles, local Party organizations were bursting and disappearing. Of course, there were Communist organizations that persisted, but Father would not support them. "We will not," he said, "join those brawlers who go to these meetings carrying red flags and holding up portraits of Stalin." At the end of July 1990, he discontinued his Party membership. Thereafter, he rarely mentioned the Party; he felt it had betrayed him for most of his life, and he found it too painful to think of.

Tatiana Kramchaninova-Serebrovska

17

Ukrainian Independence and Viktor's Last Days

Tatiana Kramchaninova-Serebrovska

The flood of reminiscences draws near...
Volodimir Sosiura (1898-1965)[58]

א

Early in 1991, the Soviet economy was collapsing. Gorbachev's *perestroika* and his political support were clearly in trouble. As the central government was failing, Ukraine faced a difficult question: "Should we continue to be a part of the Soviet Union?" We were asked to vote on the matter. Many people, ourselves included, had long understood the frailty of our Soviet government, but it was what we had known for our entire lives. We were accustomed to it. The majority of Ukrainians voted in favor of remaining in the Soviet Union. Then, on August 19, while Gorbachev was vacationing in Crimea, conservative plotters in the government and military attempted a *coup d'etat* in Moscow. Fortunately, public demonstrations and courageous democratic leaders, notably Boris Yeltsin, President of the Russian Republic, blocked the attempt. However, the *coup* was nearly successful, and this alarmed us all.

58 Published in English translation by Andrusyshen and Kirkconnell (1963, p464).

On August 22, Gorbachev returned, but there was no confidence in his government.

On August 24, President Kravchuk of Ukraine declared us to be an independent country. To see if the people agreed with him, he called for a second vote to be held in December 1991. By then *perestroika* had ended, and Gorbachev was essentially powerless. Boris Yeltsin was the new president, and the Soviet Union was beginning to break up into independent republics, the largest, of course, being Russia. The central government in Moscow was in chaos. Ties between Russia and Ukraine were already being broken, and Ukraine was moving toward independence.

But how should we vote? Father's mind was in conflict. The Soviet government had failed. Father no longer had any doubt about that. Maybe independence would bring a government that would be more responsive to the people. All over Ukraine, especially in the west, a wave of support for independence broke over the population. We were a country with immense natural resources, the most fertile farmland in the world, the largest iron and coal deposits in the Soviet Union, and more than fifty percent of its heavy industry. With all this wealth, maybe we would fare better managing our own affairs. Furthermore, Ukraine was not as large as Russia and could be governed more easily. Father agreed with his countrymen; independence might improve our lives.

Still, for cultural reasons, he hesitated to vote for separation from Russia. Ukrainians had a shared heritage with Russians and Belorussians. Marriage and family ties stretched across political borders. I myself had married a Russian. Russian literature, painting, music, and films were more varied and more insightful than their rather dreary Ukrainian counterparts. Father preferred to read Russian books, magazines, and newspapers, and to watch Russian television. He also had personal ties to the Soviet Union. He had been born in the very month that Ukraine joined the other republics to form the new Soviet state. Father and his country were the same age, and he had been its citizen all his life. He had risked that life fighting on Soviet soil throughout the Great Patriotic War. He was concerned that many politicians favored independence not for the good of Ukraine, but rather from a greedy desire to plunder Ukraine's resources. These persons, he said, were simply looking for "more and cheaper sausage." However, one cannot sit in two chairs at the same time; he knew he had to decide. In the end, he cast his vote to remain with the Motherland, but he was in the minority. Ninety percent of Ukrainians voted for independence. On December 25, 1991, Gorbachev resigned from office, and the official dissolution of the Union of Soviet Socialist Republics followed. Ukraine became an independent country.

Father was initially optimistic. Many good and honest people, including some who had been released from Soviet concentration camps, were elected to parliament. Perhaps ordinary citizens could now influence public policy. However, electing those with only good intentions was like applying a poultice to a corpse. The new parliamentarians had no experience in leadership, training in government, or knowledge of economics. They quickly discredited themselves and the idea of democracy. The changes in government had not cut deeply enough to cure the disease in our political body. The old guard simply took off their red Communist hats and wrapped themselves in the yellow and blue Ukrainian flag. Those who had mismanaged Chernobyl and were guilty of the cover up remained in power. By resorting to devilish tricks, they adroitly resisted democratic changes. Very soon, well-meaning politicians left the political stage and disappeared from our television screens. We were left with a corrupt and deceitful government. Greedy politicians sold state enterprises and pocketed the money. They robbed the state banks, swindling us and millions of others of our lifetime savings. Father's worst fears became reality.

The corruption at the top caused poverty at the bottom. Many lost their jobs. Those of us lucky enough to have work went months without pay, and when we received our salary, it had been reduced. By 1993, the nation's economy was in free-fall. By 1994, our wages were less than one fifth of their value before independence. Food was scarce and inflation was rampant. Father's fishing was no longer a pastime, but a necessity, and his famous hot fish soup became a staple of our diet. Remarkably, as money grew scarce, Father grew resolute: "Only the weak and nervous expect God to protect them from disaster": this was ever Barbara's credo. For her, faith in the non-existent, the invisible, and the intangible weakened human resolve, lessened will power, and reduced inner strength. Like his mother during the famine and the war, Father was a pillar of strength for the family. Rather than expressing bitterness at our failing government, Father emphasized our strengths. Boguz would have been proud of him. True, we had little money, but we had ourselves, our health, and our *dacha*.

Our *dacha* in Poltava became our kitchen garden—it was essential to our food supply and to our survival. Father went to work on the *dacha* with the deliberation of a peasant. Now his retirement had purpose: he was feeding his family once more, as he had in the Donbass on Progress Farm. During the growing season, he and Mother lived at the *dacha,* and Alexander and I joined them on weekends. There was so much to be done there: cultivating the vegetables, caring for the fruit trees, and digging a storage cellar. In the autumn, Mother and I canned hundreds of jars of fruit and vegetables. These fed us through the winter. Many in Kiev did as we did, and on Friday evenings, at the end of the regular workweek, there was a curiously depressing sight. Rushing to the trains was the flower of our nation: literally thousands of intellectual men and women dressed in shabby work clothes, bringing with them homemade wheelbarrows. Out of work, or with earnings so meager that they could not buy enough food, they had to farm the land. We were among these hordes.

Our *dacha* had but one room and a kitchen, but it had been sturdily built a half century ago. The thick stone walls plastered with white lime inside and out and a roof made of slate helped the house stay cool on hot summer days. A well supplied the water. This *dacha* brought us more than food—it brought us together. When our three children were small, they, with Father and Mother, could sleep in the main room, while Alexander and I slept in the kitchen. Later, the children slept in the shed. Though the dacha was small, it served us well.

Viktor, age seventy-four, putting the roof on the new house at the dacha.

Still, we needed more room, and building a new house from floor to roof from scavenged second-hand material was a great adventure for us. It was what Father enjoyed most, and he threw himself into it with great enthusiasm. When school was out, the children joined in. They also watered and weeded the garden, and in autumn they gathered the harvest. If the *dacha* was necessary for our budget, it was also wonderful for our children. They spent their days under the sky and learned to esteem village life. They learned to value hard work, and in this their grandparents were experts. I cannot measure the collective satisfaction around the dinner table when we opened the jars containing the fruit and vegetables that our three generations had grown. When there was a guest, without fail we would say, "Try these apples from our tree," or "We made this wine from our grapes." The pride came not only from the produce, but also from producing it together. The necessity of growing our own food strengthened our family.

The fiftieth anniversary of Victory Day, May 9, 1995, was a grand anniversary. Wearing the campaign ribbons of the twelve battles in which he had participated, Father, with his guests and grandchildren, watched the great parade along Krechatik Street through the center of Kiev. We women stayed at home to prepare the feast. After the parade, we and our guests celebrated with vodka, many toasts, and much singing. Father did not know that he was to receive the anniversary medal for "Victory in the Great Patriotic War" in honor of this occasion. It commemorated his heroic service and had been delivered from Moscow directly to his home. When the moment arrived—to his great surprise—the medal was brought out. According to our custom, Mother dipped the medal into vodka, proudly pinned it to his breast, and kissed and embraced her personal hero. As they waltzed around the room, there were no dry eyes at the table.

Viktor on 9 May 1995, the fiftieth anniversary of Victory Day.

Two more years passed. Father and Mother had never had a proper wedding celebration. In February of 1947, during the privations of the immediate postwar period, they had celebrated their marriage underground in a spare and dreary military dugout. The ravages of war were too recent for Father's military comrades to stage a really festive event. My parents' fiftieth wedding anniversary provided the opportunity for the wedding celebration that they richly deserved, but never had. For the occasion, we made sure that Mother had a proper, traditional bridal veil and that Father had the special fiancé flower for his buttonhole. All the family took part in the preparation. The granddaughters, Zoya and Nadia, prepared a certificate and a chocolate medal. Father's brother, Gregory, recited the poetry he had composed. Accompanied by Lena or myself at the piano and Zoya and Nadia on guitars, everyone took part in singing in four- and five-part harmonies, as usual. It was a fitting climax to the years since 1940, when Barbara had called to the girls graduating from Zhitomyr High School: "Which of you will be my daughter-in-law," and Father's brother, Alexander, had shouted: "There she is, Maria Rudenko!"

Viktor and Maria on their fiftieth wedding anniversary, February 1997.

Indeed, here she still was. Though she had grown old, she was still the same kind and beautiful person she had always been. What remained of that tenth-grade boy, Viktor, who had shared a school desk with a quiet girl with an "enchanting smile and reddish-golden hair"? He had liked her, but had thought she could not guess his feelings. Not only had she guessed, but she had remained true to that tenth-grade boy throughout the war, and through the hardships and struggles that followed, and he had been true to her. Their lives had not been easy. The stresses, though enormous, had been mostly from outside the marriage, not from within. Together, Viktor and Maria had survived.

Family assembled at the fiftieth wedding anniversary. Seated, from left to right: Maria in her bridal veil, Viktor, Tatiana (elder daughter of Viktor and Maria), Alexander Serebrovsky (Tatiana's husband). Standing, from left to right: Maria (Lena's daughter), Lena (younger daughter of Viktor and Maria), Nadiya (Tatiana's younger daughter), Aloysha (Lena's son), Gregory (Viktor's youngest brother), Zoya (Tatiana's elder daughter), Ludmila (Gregory's wife).

Father had been losing weight. One day, late in 1998, he returned from his annual checkup at the hospital for veterans with the news that an ultrasound scan had found something wrong with his liver. An examination at the Cancer Institute confirmed our worst fears. Father understood that he would not live long. It was a time for reminiscence. For years, Mother had filed away the family artifacts in an infinitely expandable maroon paperboard accordion file. Even mounting the photographs in two large albums had not reduced the bulk of her treasures. With the help of this trove, the pictures, letters, medals, father's memoirs, and other memorabilia, they recalled their childhoods and their life together. They had lived through the entire life of the Soviet Union. In their youth, they had seen it rise, and in old age, they had seen it fall.

Now I could see how Father felt. He loved his country. He was grateful for the education it had provided him in literature, history, mathematics and science. His education in aeronautics had allowed him to support his family, but he knew that he had been among the more fortunate. Life had shown him that the government was inefficient and not committed to the people. Seeing these failures were the most painful lessons of his lifetime. Surely what he had learned as a child, that people should work and share, was not wrong— it was only difficult. Whether Communism would ever be attempted again, he did not know, but if it were, people must be allowed to work for their own benefit as well as for the common good. He commented that governments never seem to get it quite right when balancing individual initiative against needs of the many. Proof of success, he said, would be an improved life for ordinary people, not a display of power, but he did not know how to make it work.

In these final months, Father also thought about religion. To some extent, his beliefs were those of his parents. As a woman of her times, Barbara had marched in step with the Soviet way of life. When she was a child, her parents had forced her to go to church every week to pray, but she did not believe in God. Although she would occasionally go to church at Christmas or Easter, it was "just not to be different from other people." When there were scandals regarding members of the clergy, whom she regarded as parasites, she made fun of them. Her faith was in Nature and in the power of the universe. Panteley shared her opinions.

Father was more inclusive. Something of the boy remained in him from the nights on Progress Farm when he had lain on his back looking at the Milky Way. On the musical nights in high school when he and Maria had looked up at the night sky, they had "marveled at the constellations and the planets." Father retained a sense of wonder at the vastness of the universe; it had even led him into flying. In the presence of Grandpa Boguz, he had experienced a calm that transcended the physical world. Father felt that somewhere in the universe there might be a supreme intelligence, or something uniquely capable of creating suns, planets, and life. Although he did not believe that human prayers could reach this intelligence, or that it would change the circumstances of one's life, he could accept that prayer was a kind of meditation that provided "medicine for the soul." It could help one find an inner peace and a healing of spiritual wounds. At the end of his life, when he knew that the cancer was killing him, he wondered about the afterlife and asked for a priest to be called. His struggle with his beliefs, both political and religious, remained with him until the end.

In the company of his family, Father accepted his approaching death. There was no self-pity, nor were there complaints about his lot. If surgery were proposed, he planned to refuse. When he became bedridden, he didn't talk about himself or his illness. His concern was Maria's welfare. He died on June 17, 1999 in his seventy-seventh year, having lived a life of service to his family, his friends, his colleagues, and his country. In this he had persevered; perhaps that was enough.

For us, we remember his life, and the countless lives of others who faced with courage Ukraine's turbulent twentieth century. Each year on 23 February, previously known as "The Day of the Soviet Army" and now as "The Day of The Motherland Defenders," we recall vivid memories of those who died for our country. It is also a day for introspection in our own lives. It is an emotional day and it affects us deeply. Each year, at about noon on this day, someone from the district administration rings our doorbell and brings us a gift—a plastic bag containing a bottle of vodka, a loaf of brown bread, a piece of corned lard, and a triangular letter of congratulation. When Father was alive, everyone in our family assembled at his home to celebrate this day. Now we are only three: Mother, Alexander, and I. Mother answers the door and receives the gift. We fill our glasses with vodka. One glass, covered with a slice of the brown bread, is placed before Father's portrait. It is our tradition to honor an airman who will never again return from his mission. Then we drink to Father and to all the patriots who perished for our "radiant future."

It's a pity that our children can so rarely join us, but for them, life takes its normal course. They follow their own experience and make their own memories. For now, I am content to have Alexander and Mother with me. But what of the future, when Alexander and I are old? Sometimes I dare not think of it. Yet Father began these memoirs with the words, "Without the past there is no future." We draw strength from our past, knowing how older generations struggled and how they endured. If the future is difficult for us, we will examine and re-examine our past. Our future journey may not be easy, but our parents and their parents showed us that we can face it with courage.

Tatiana Kramchaninova-Serebrovska

Notes:

1. Published in English translation by Andrusyshen and Kirkconnell (1963, p464).

APPENDIX A

EXCERPT FROM THE SECRET PROTOCOL BETWEEN GERMANY AND THE SOVIET UNION AS SIGNED IN MOSCOW, 23 AUGUST 1939

"Article II. In the event of a territorial and political rearrangement of the areas belonging to the Polish state, the spheres of influence of Germany and the U.S.S.R. shall be bounded approximately by the line of the rivers Narev, Vistula, and San.

The question of whether the interests of both parties make desirable the maintenance of an independent Polish State and how such a state should be bounded can only be definitely determined in the course of further political developments.

In any event, both governments will resolve this question by means of a friendly agreement." (Leonhard 1989, p 40-41)

APPENDIX B

EXCERPT FROM MAJOR PUSSEP'S ARTICLE PUBLISHED IN *WINGS OF THE MOTHERLAND*, JANUARY 1986

"Before our departure from Washington we had learned that the Nazis were already informed about our meeting with President Roosevelt of the USA and that they had plans to intercept our airplane during the return flight. Moreover, our command had made the decision to fly over the European continent. So, in order to mislead the enemy, we decided to publish in the newspapers the report about the signing of the agreement and a summary of the text. The fascists swallowed the bait—they decided our delegation had already returned to Moscow. As a result, our 'corridor' opened, and we returned home using exactly this route."

APPENDIX C

LETTER FROM KUZNETSOV FAMILY TO ZHELEZNODOROZHNIY DISTRICT SOCIAL SECURITY COUNCIL, KIEV

"I, Efrosinja Nikitina, the teacher of Tjunino high school, who lives in Tjunino village of Dubovski Rayon, in the region of Bryansk Oblast, and I, Peter Kuznetsov, foreman on the railroad, who lives at the same place, verify the following:

During the Patriotic War, the German aggressors temporarily occupied our region. On the night of 27 August 1943 the Soviet pilots bombed German troops at the railway junction of Roslavl. One of our planes was shot down during the fight and dropped, burning, into the forest near the rail siding at Schepet. The airplane was destroyed by fire. The charred remains of six crewmembers of this large bomber were buried near the airplane on the following day by one of our local peasants. Our family picked up an airman from the stricken airplane. This was Viktor Kramchaninov, a crewman with the 'Hero of the Soviet Union,' Major Vihorev.

Kramchaninov had received severe wounds to his face, head, hands, and legs. His eyes were red from a hemorrhage suffered on impact with the ground. His face and arms were blistered from burns, and large bruises covered much of his body. We hid him from the Germans and their collaborators in a forest near the village.

For seven days he lay in the forest. Our family—brothers Basil [who later perished], *Anton, Peter, and Viktor, and I and my sister-in-law Maria Maljutina—brought him food, looked after him, and treated his injuries. The threat of death hovered over us all, since the Germans shot partisans, Soviet airmen, and anyone who hid them.*

When Kramchaninov recovered he asked to be linked with the partisans. In September 1943 our brothers Basil and Anton brought two guerrilla fighters to him, and they took him to their partisan squad. After he recovered, Kramchaninov participated in battle operations on railroads and on the Warsaw highway. He then traversed the front lines with a group of partisans and took with him two captive German officers who later gave important military information to Soviet troops.

In 1944, after the liberation of our region, we received a letter from Kramchaninov at the front, in which he notified us that he continued to fight the Germans by air.

Also in 1944 we received a letter from the air force unit at 'Field Mail 13730,' in which the commander thanked our family for saving the life of airman Kramchaninov after he was shot down during the fulfillment of a battle task. This letter is stored in Tjunino high school."

The above letter was signed by E.F. Nikitina and P.F. Kuznetsov of Tjunino Village Council of the Deputies of the Working Masses, and by P.D. Abramov, Chairman.

At the end of the letter was a hand-written statement:

"Everything in the above document is true. In the period of temporary occupation by the Germans of the given terrain, I lived here, in the region where the airplane (on which Kramchaninov flew*) was destroyed."*

The statement was signed:

"B.Prozorkevich, teacher of Tjunino elementary school, nowadays a pensioner."

APPENDIX D

LETTER FROM ALFRED ROSENBERG, NAZI MINISTER OF EASTERN OCCUPIED TERRITORIES, TO GENERAL KEITEL OF THE GERMAN ARMY

28 FEBRUARY 1942

This letter from Alfred Rosenberg, Nazi Minister of Eastern Occupied Territories, to General Keitel of the German Army, sought more humane treatment of Soviet prisoners, but it did not prevent Rosenberg from being executed as a war criminal in 1946.

> "...*The fate of Soviet prisoners of war in Germany is...a tragedy of the greatest dimensions. Of the 3.6 million prisoners of war, today only several hundred thousand are completely fit for work. A large portion of them have starved to death or have died of exposure... Thousands have also succumbed to typhus. It is obvious that the feeding of such masses of prisoners of war will encounter difficulties. Nevertheless, had there been a certain amount of understanding for the aims of German policy, death and demoralization on such a scale could have been avoided. For example, according to the reports we have received,...the civilian (Soviet) population was completely prepared to supply food to the prisoners of war. Several understanding camp commanders followed this route with success. In the majority of cases, however, the camp commandants forbade the civilian population from supplying the prisoners of war with food and preferred to leave them to die of starvation. The civilian population was*

also not allowed to give food to the prisoners of war during their march to the camps. Indeed, in many cases, when hungry and exhausted prisoners of war could no longer continue with the march, they were shot before the eyes of the horrified population, and their bodies were left to lie where they fell. In many camps no shelter at all was provided for the prisoners of war. They lay there exposed to the rain and snow. They were not even provided with the equipment to dig themselves foxholes or caves.... Utterances have been heard, such as: 'The more of the prisoners who die, the better it is for us.'...Finally one must also mention the shootings of prisoners of war, which...are devoid of any political sense... One encounters the view that the peoples become increasingly inferior the further east one goes. If the Poles must be treated harshly then the same applies on a much larger scale to the Ukrainians, Belorussians, Russians,..." (Boshyk 1986, p 176).

APPENDIX E

TREATMENT OF UKRAINIANS UNDER GERMAN OCCUPATION IN SECOND WORLD WAR

On 11 August 1941, much of Ukraine became ruled by *Reichskommissar* Erich Koch, Hitler's personal appointee (Manning 1951). Reportedly, Koch's August 1942 speech in Rivne stated, in part, that "The goal of our work must be that the Ukrainians work for Germany and not that we insure the happiness of the people. … The food situation in Germany is serious. …grain must be procured from Ukraine…[and] the feeding of the Ukrainian civilian population is of absolutely no concern. …The *Führer* has demanded three million tonnes of grain from Ukraine …" (Boshyk, 1986, p179).

Koch said of himself, "I am a brutal dog, ...[who intends] to suck from Ukraine all the goods we can get hold of without consideration...of Ukrainians. …If I find a Ukrainian who is worthy of sitting at the same table with me, I must have him shot" (Krawchenko, 1986, p24, 29). Ukraine suffered enormously in World War II. Of approximately forty million people, seven million to thirteen million, depending on the estimate, died in the War. Even using the lower estimate, the number exceeds the population loss by Germany, Japan, Italy, France, the British Commonwealth, and the United States combined. American correspondent Edgar Snow, who visited Ukraine in 1943 and 1945, was so impressed by the enormity of human and property losses that he wrote for the *Saturday Evening Post*: "The Allies won the war, but Ukraine paid the bill" (Gregorovich, 1995, p1).

APPENDIX F

CHRONOLOGY OF NATIONAL AND INTERNATIONAL EVENTS (1914 – 1991) IN RELATION TO THE KRAMCHANINOV FAMILY

1914	In August World War I began between the Triple Entente (Britain, France and Russia) and the Triple Alliance (Germany, Austria-Hungary and Italy).
1917	In March, under pressure from the military, Czar Nicholas II renounced the throne of Russia, and the Provisional Government was established.
1917.	On 7 November by the new calendar (25 October by the old one), the Bolsheviks overthrew the Provisional Government in the "Great October Socialist Revolution." Under Lenin, the Bolsheviks established the Congress of Soviets.
1918	The Brest-Litovsk Treaty was signed in March, ending Russian/Soviet participation in World War I.
1918	Beginning of the Soviet Civil War between the Bolsheviks and the anti-Bolsheviks.
1918	Czar Nicholas II (1868-1918) and his family were murdered by the Bolsheviks.
1920	Civil War victory for the Bolsheviks.

1920-23	Famine killed at least three million and perhaps as many as ten million people in the Soviet republics.
1922	On 30 December four socialist republics—Russia, Ukraine, and the Transcaucasian and Belorussian Soviet Socialist Republics—were united as the Union of Soviet Socialist Republics, also called the Soviet Union.
1923	In March what previously had been western Ukraine, including the city of L'viv, was annexed to Poland.
1924	Vladimir Lenin died on 21 January.
1928	Josef Stalin assumed total power in the Soviet Union.
1929	Stalin introduced his Five Year Plan, which began the forced collectivization of agriculture.
1931-33	Famine in Ukraine.
1933	Adolph Hitler (1889-1945) became Chancellor of Germany.
1934	Hitler assumed total power in what became Nazi Germany.
1939.	On 20 August a "Commercial Treaty" was signed, whereby the Soviet Union sent grain and raw materials to Germany.
1939	On 23 August the Nazi-Soviet Non-Aggression Treaty was signed, paving the way for World War II.
1939	On 1 September Germany invaded Poland. On 3 September France and Britain declared war on Germany. On 17 September Soviet armies entered eastern Poland and western Ukraine.

1939 On 28 September a protocol was signed which established the boundaries between Germany and the Soviet Union. The formerly Polish city of L'viv was incorporated into Ukraine.

1941 In March the Lend-Lease Act was passed, whereby the United States would lend or lease some seven billion dollars of weapons and other aid to any countries President Roosevelt might designate.

1941 On 22 June more than three million German troops invaded the Soviet Union.

1941 On 30 June the German Army entered L'viv *(Maria's family home).*

1941 In July the German army occupied Zhitomyr *(Viktor's family home).*

1941 On 19 September German forces captured Kiev, and by 26 September had taken more than 600,000 Soviet soldiers, many of whom were Ukrainian.

1941 On 16 October German troops occupied Odessa.

1941 On 24 October the German Army captured Kharkiv.

1941 In September Leningrad was besieged by German troops.

1941 On 7 December the Japanese attacked Pearl Harbor. The following day the United States declared war on Germany, Japan, and Italy.

1942 In April Hitler directed forces to the Caucasus to secure the oil fields for Germany.

1942 In May and June Molotov, the Soviet Foreign Minister, flew to London and Washington. Roosevelt promised military supplies to the Soviet Union and that the United States and Britain would invade Europe in 1942.

1942 In July the fall of Sevastopol gave the German Army control of the Crimea.

1942 In August Churchill traveled to Moscow to give Stalin the news that Britain and the United States could not open a second front in Europe as Molotov had been promised, and that supply convoys to the Soviet Union were being suspended because of German submarine activity.

1942 In August German troops reached the outskirts of Stalingrad (now Volgograd), beginning the largest battle of World War II.

1942 In September the German Army invading the Caucasus was stopped at the Terek River.

1942 In November Soviet forces encircled German forces at Stalingrad.

1943 In February the German Army at Stalingrad surrendered.

1943 In April Marshal Zhukov, the Military Commander over the Soviet Western front, informed Stalin that the German Army would attack Kursk from Orel in the north and from Belgorod in the south.

1943 On 5 July the German attack on Kursk began.

1943 On 9 July British and United States forces invaded Sicily.

1943 On 12 July Hitler ordered an end to the German offensive at Kursk, and their army began to withdraw.

1943 On 6 November Kiev was retaken by the Soviet Army. The population had decreased from 900,000 to less than 200,000.

1943 In December Zhitomyr and Lubni *(where Maria's family now lived)* were liberated by the Soviet Army.

1944 In January the siege of Leningrad was broken.

1944 On 6 June Allied forces invaded German-occupied France.

1944 On 27 July the Soviet Army retook L'viv.

1945 On 9 May the unconditional surrender of Germany ended World War II in Europe.

1945 On 6 August the United States dropped an atomic bomb on Hiroshima, Japan.

1945 On 8 August the Soviet Union declared war on Japan.

1945. On 9 August the Soviet Army invaded Manchuria. The United States dropped an atomic bomb on Nagasaki.

1945. On 15 August the United States accepted the Japanese surrender.

1945 On 2 September Japan signed an official surrender document, signaling the end of World War II.

1953 In March Stalin died, and Nikita Khrushchev became General Secretary of the Central Committee of the Communist Party.

1962 Alexander Solzhenitsyn's novel, *One Day in the Life of Ivan Denisovich*, became available to Soviet citizens.

1964 In October Leonid Brezhnev replaced Khrushchev as General Secretary of the Party.

1973 Mohammed Daoud declared Afghanistan a republic with himself as President.

1978 In April a bloody Communist coup led by Nur Mohammed Taraki took over the Afghan government.

1979 In Iran, Afghanistan's westernmost neighbor, the Ayatollah Khomeini, a radical Islamic mullah, deposed the Shah of Iran, and probably fomented the March riot against the Taraki Soviet-style government in Herat, Afghanistan.

1979 In September a military coup in Afghanistan by Hafizullah Amin deposed and killed Taraki.

1979. In December the Soviet Army invaded Afghanistan.

1982 Brezhnev died and was replaced by Yuri Andropov, former head of the KGB.

1984 Andropov died and was replaced by Konstantin Chernenko.

1985 Chernenko died and was replaced by Mikhail Gorbachev, who instituted policies of *glasnost* (openness) and *perestroika* (restructuring).

1986 On 26 April reactor four at the Chernobyl Nuclear Power Plant exploded.

1986. On 3 May the Soviet government officially declared that a disaster had occurred at Chernobyl.

1989 The Soviet Union withdrew from Afghanistan.

1991 In June Boris Yeltsin (1931-2007) was elected President of the Russian Federation.

1991 On 24 August, alarmed by the attempted coup against Gorbachev's government, President Kravchuk declared Ukraine an independent country.

1991 On 1 December Ukrainians voted overwhelmingly for independence from the Soviet Union.

1991. On 21 December Russia, Ukraine, and Belarus signed a protocol establishing the Commonwealth of Independent States.

1991 On 25 December Gorbachev resigned from office.

1991 On 26 December the Soviet Union was dissolved.

BIBLIOGRAPHY/REFERENCE LIST

Alliluyeva, Svetlana. *Twenty Letters to a Friend.* Translated by Priscilla J. McMillan. New York: Harper & Row, 1967.

Andrusyshen, C.H. and W. Kirkconnell. *The Ukrainian Poets: 1189-1962.* Toronto: University of Toronto Press, 1963.

Anwar, Raja. *The Tragedy of Afghanistan: a First Hand Account.* London: Verso, 1988.

Aslund, Anders and Georges de Ménil. *Economic Reform in Ukraine: The Unfinished Agenda.* Armonk, New York: 2000.

Ausubel, J.H. 1992. "Chernobyl after Perestroika: reflections on a recent visit." http://phe.rockefeller.edu/Chernobyl.

Berelowitch, A. "Russia: an unfinished job." http://www.unesco.org/courier/1999_12/uk/dossier/tx106.html

Berezhkov, V.M. *At Stalin's Side.* New York: Birch Lane Press Book; Carol Publishing Group, 1994.

Bromage, E. *Molotov: The Story of an Era.* London: Peter Owen, Ltd., 1956.

Chuev, F. *Molotov Remembers: Inside Kremlin Politics, Conversations with Felix Chuev.* Chicago: Ivan R. Ree, Inc, 1993.

Churchill, Winston S. *The Second World War: Volume IV, The Hinge of Fate.* Boston: Houghton Mifflin Co., 1950. (Paperback edition, 1978)

Coleman, F. *The Decline and Fall of the Soviet Empire.* New York: St. Martin's Press, 1996.

Collins, Joseph J. *The Soviet Invasion of Afghanistan.* D.C. Heath and Company, 1986.

Conquest, R. *The Harvest of Sorrow.* New York: Oxford University Press, 1986.

Cordovez, D., and S.S. Harrison. *Out of Afghanistan: The Inside Story of Soviet Withdrawal.* New York: Oxford University Press, 1995.

Cunningham, H.S. "1999. Pavlik Morozov 1918(?)-1932." http://www.cyberussr.com/rus/morozov.html.

Dementriev, G.P. "Union of Soviet Socialist Republics". In *Encyclopædia Britannica.* London: William Benton, Publisher, 1967.

Druzhnikov, Y. *Informer 001.* New Brunswick, NJ: Transaction Publishers, 1994.

Duffy, P., *A. Kandalov. Tupolev - The Man and His Aircraft.* London: Airlife, 1996.

Essame, H. "Sicily (1943)", in, *The Mammoth Book of Battles,* ed., J.E. Lewis, New York: Carroll & Graf, Inc., 1995.

Ewans, Martin. *Afghanistan.* New York: Harper Collins Publishers, 2002.

Figes, O. *A People's Tragedy: a History of the Russian Revolution.* New York: Viking Press, 1996.

Fisher, H.H. *The Famine in Soviet Russia 1919-1923.* New York: The Macmillan Co., 1927.

Fitzpatrick, S. *Everyday Stalinism: Ordinary Life in Extraordinary Times: Soviet Russia in the 1930s.* New York: Oxford University Press, 1999.

Garrard, J and C. Garrard. *Inside the Soviet Writer's Union.* New York: The Free Press, Macmillan, Inc., 1990.

Getty, J.A., and R.T. Manning. *Stalinist Terror*. Cambridge University Press, Cambridge, 1993.

Ghaus, Abdul Samad. *The Fall of Afghanistan*. London: Pergamon-Brassey's International Defense Publishers Inc., 1988.

Girardet, Edward. *Afghanistan: the Soviet War*. New York: St. Martin's Press, 1985.

Golder, F. A., and L. Hutchinson. *On the Trail of the Russian Famine*. Palo Alto, Calif.: Stanford University Press, 1927.

Gordon, Y., and D. Khazanov. *Soviet Combat Aircraft of the Second World War*. Volume two. Leicester, England: Midland Publishing Ltd., 1999.

Gregorovich, A. 2000. "Black famine in Ukraine 1932-33. A struggle for existence." http://www.infoukes.com/history/famine/gregorovich.

Gregorovich, A. 1995. "World War II in Ukraine: The Ukrainian experience in World War II with a brief survey of Ukraine's population loss of 10 million." http://www.infoukes.com/history/ww2.

Hannah, J. (http://www.24sqnassociation.royalairforce.net/issue8.htm)

Hart, B.H.L. "World War II, H. The German-Russian War." In *Encyclopædia Britannica*. London: William Benton, Publisher, 1967.

Havin, A.F. *U rulia industrii (At the Rudder of Industry: Feature Stories)*. Moscow: Politizdat, 1968, p 197-230. (In Russian)

Isby, D.C. *War in a Distant Country - Afghanistan: Invasion and Resistance*. London: Arms and Armour Press, 1989.

Johnson, C. *Narrative Poems by Alexander Pushkin and by Mikhail Lermontov*. New York: Random House, 1983.

Koslow, J. *The Despised and the Damned: The Russian Peasant through the Ages.* New York: Macmillan Company, 1972.

Krawchenko, B. "Soviet Ukraine under Nazi Occupation, 1941-4." In: *Ukraine during World War II: History and Its Aftermath,* ed. Y. Boshyk, (Edmonton: Canadian Institute of Ukrainian Studies, 1986).

Khrushchev, N, E. Crankshaw, and S. Talbott. *Khrushchev Remembers.* Little Brown and Company, Boston, 1970.

Lee, A.W. "World War II, J. The Sicilian Campaign, May-August 1943." In *Encyclopædia Britannica.* London: William Benton, Publisher, 1967.

Leonard, W. *Betrayal: The Hitler-Stalin Pact of 1939.* New York: St. Martin's Press, 1989.

Lermontov, M. "The Demon," in: *Narrative Poems by Alexander Pushkin and Mikhail Lermontov.* Translated by Charles Johnson. New York: Random House, 1983.

Leslie, R.F., "Russo-Turkish Wars." In *Encyclopædia Britannica.* London: William Benton, Publisher, 1967.

Levytsky, B. *The Stalinist Terror in the Thirties: Documentation from the Soviet Press.* Aleksandr Pavlovich Serebrovsky, p461-463. Stanford, California: Hoover Institution Press, 1974.

Lewin, M. *Russian Peasants and Soviet Power: A Study of Collectivization.* Translated by I. Nove and J. Boiggart. Evanston, Illinois: Northwestern University Press, 1968.

Lindstrom, T.S. *A Concise History of Russian Literature, Vol. II from 1900 to the Present.* New York: The Gotham Library of the New York University Press, 1978.

Lyons, E. *Herbert Hoover: a Biography*. Garden City, New York: Doubleday & Company, Inc., 1964.

Magnus, R.H., and E. Naby. *Afghanistan: Mullah, Marx, and Mujahid*. Boulder, Colorado: Westview Press, 1998.

Maning, C.A. *Twentieth-Century Ukraine*. New York: Bookman Associates, 1951.

Marshall, G.C. "World War II, VI. The Cost." In *Encyclopædia Britannica*. London: William Benton, Publisher, 1967.

Mould, R.F. *Chernobyl Record: The Definitive History of the Chernobyl Catastrophe*. Bristol, U.K.: Institute of Physics Publishing, 2000.

Nawroz, M.Y., and L.W. Grau. "The Soviet War in Afghanistan: History and Harbinger of Future War?" Fort Leavenworth, Kansas: United States Army, Foreign Military Studies Office. May 9, 2002. http://www.bdg.minsk.by/cegi/N2/Afg/Waraf

Nowarra, H.J., and G.R. Duval. *Russian Civil and Military Aircraft 1884-1969*. Harleyford, 1976.

Orwell, G. *Animal Farm*. New York: Harcourt, Brace and Co., 1946.

Overy, R. *Why the Allies Won*. New York: Norton & Co., 1996.

Pushkin A. "Onegin's Journey," in: *Narrative Poems by Alexander Pushkin and Mikhail Lermontov*. Translated by Charles Johnson. New York: Random House, 1983.

Pushkin, A. *Boris Godunov*. http://www.blackmask.com/books73c/brsgdhtm#1_0_10, 2002

Pushkin, A. *Boris Godunov*. Russian text with translation and notes by Philip L. Barbour. New York: Columbia University Press, 1953.

Read, A., and D. Fisher. *The Deadly Embrace: Hitler, Stalin, and the Nazi-Soviet Pact, 1939-1941*. New York: W.W. Norton & Co., 1988.

Reese, R. "The Red Army and the Great Purges," in: *Stalinist Terror: new perspectives*, eds. J.A. Getty and R.T. Manning, New York: Cambridge University Press, 1993.

Reeve, W. "Afghanistan's turbulent history." *World: South Asia*, Friday, 28 September, 2001. http://news.bbc.co.uk

Rosenberg, A. "Letter from Alfred Rosenberg to General Keitel on Nazi Treatment of Soviet Prisoners of war." In: *Ukraine during World War II: History and Its Aftermath*, p 176-177, ed. Y. Boshyk, Edmonton: Canadian Institute of Ukrainian Studies, 1986.

Ruffle, R.J. Group Leader, Russian Aviation Research Group, Air-Britain, International Association of Aviation Historians. (Personal communication to JTR, 8 October, 2001).

Sarin, O., and L. Dvoretsky. *The Afghan Syndrome: the Soviet Union's Vietnam*. Novato, Calif.: Presidio Press, 1993.

Service, R. *A History of Twentieth-Century Russia.* Cambridge, Mass.: Harvard University Press, 1997.

Shlapentokh, Vladimir. *A Normal Totalitarian Society: How the Soviet Union functioned and how it collapsed.* Armonk, New York, 2001.

Sherwood, R.E. *Roosevelt and Hopkins: an Intimate History.* New York: Harper & Brothers, 1948, 1950.

Smogorzewski, K.M., "Union of Soviet Socialist Republics: VI. Administration and Social Conditions." In *Encyclopædia Britannica*. London: William Benton, Publisher, 1967.

Solzhenitsyn, A. *Gulag Archipelago: An Experiment in Literary Investigation*. New York: Harper & Row, Publishers, 1973.

Solzhenitsyn, A. *One Day in the Life of Ivan Denisovich*. New York: Signet Classic, Penguin Books USA, 1963.

Solzhenitsyn, Alexander, biography. http://msms.essortment.com/aleksandrsolz_rdmg.htm, PageWise, Inc, 2001.

Sonnevytsky, L. Brama. "History of Ukraine." http://www.brama.com/ukraine/history/century20.html, 2002.

Soskice, JM. *Poems by Nikolai Nekrasov*. Westport, Conn.: Hyperion Press, Inc., 1977.

Strayer, Robert. *Why Did the Soviet Union Collapse?: Understanding Historical Changes*. Arfmonk, New York: M.E. Sharpe, 1998.

Surface, F.M., and R.L. Bland. *American Food in the World War and Reconstruction Period*. Palo Alto, Calif.: Stanford University Press, 1931.

Urban, Mark L. *War in Afghanistan*. New York: St. Martin's Press, Inc., 1988.

Wikipedia the Free Encyclopedia. 2002. Perestroika. http://wikipedia.org/wiki/perestroika.

Wykes, A. "Kursk", in *The Mammoth Book of Battles*, ed., J.E. Lewis, New York: Carroll & Graf, Inc., 1995.

Young, C.T. "de Havilland D.H. Flamingo." http://www.geocities.com/ctyoung57/DH95_1.html, 2000.

Young, C.T. Personal communication to JTR, 22 June, 2001.

Zhukov, G.K. *Marshal Zhukov's Greatest Battles.* Translated by T. Shabad, ed, H.E. Salisbury. New York: Harper & Row, 1969.